Circle of Awareness

Circle of Awareness

Using the body as a mirror for thoughts:
a psychotherapeutic approach

Willem Fonteijn

Warden Press

© 2016 Willem Fonteijn

ISBN:
Paperback: 978-94-92004-37-6
E-book (Epub): 978-94-92004-38-3
E-book (Kindle): 978-94-92004-39-0

Cover design: Sander Pinkse, Amsterdam
Photo author: Rien Bazen, Amsterdam
Interior design and lay-out: Elgraphic bv, Vlaardingen
This edition published by Warden Press, Amsterdam

for Sultana

Table of contents

Preface

Identifying, challenging, and correcting dysfunctional opinions and behaviors is the core business of Cognitive Behavior Therapy (CBT). Recent developments such as Mindfulness Behavioral Cognitive Therapy (MBCT), Acceptance and Commitment Therapy (ACT) and Meta-Cognitive Therapy (MCT) emphasize replacement of the challenging aspect by awareness and acceptance (which are, in my opinion, different ways of challenging). These new developments have been identified by some authors as 'third generation CBT'.

Willem Fonteijn is an independent and creative cognitive behavioral therapist. Being different from MBCT, ACT or MCT, his *Circle of Awareness* is all about awareness and acceptance. The 'modus operandi' of the *Circle of Awareness* is illustrated by descriptions of a huge range of real patients and clients with recognizable and more or less prototypical problems like panic, addiction and pain. They offer a rich source of inspiration for those psychotherapists who take an interest in awareness and acceptance, as well as for persons who take interest into enlarging their own personal awareness. As a 'COMET therapist' my own interest was particularly caught by the role attributed to the body and its motor and physiologic responses in Fonteijn's work.

At the moment, my personal positive impressions of the *Circle of Awareness* are based on the personal experiences and anecdotic reports of the author and his patients and clients. While I expect these experiences to trigger the interest of many others including practicing therapists as well, I hope that these same therapists are interested in the results of future studies that should investigate the *Circle of Awareness'* efficacy in a more scientific empirical way.

Prof. dr. Kees Korrelboom, clinical psychologist and psychotherapist.

Introduction

There is more wisdom in your body than in your deepest philosophy. (Friedrich Nietzsche)

In this book we circle around one topic only: awareness. All the issues raised and explored in this book point in one direction: awareness. This book is all about awareness. What started as an experiential group training approach resulted in a practice of awareness. This book can be used as a practical guide to applying awareness in daily life. Whatever comes to awareness and is attended to in a friendly and accepting way will flourish and grow. Several topics are explored from different perspectives. They are all rooted in a common ground: awareness. Small adjustments will be made for exploring topics in a different way, and even those adjustments are expressions of the same process; awareness exploring awareness.

The circle of awareness is an invitation to self-exploration. People sit together in a circle. Then one of the participants steps into the circle and raises an issue of importance. The other participants focus their attention on the person in the circle. The circle works as an open space revealing the hidden features of the issue.

The trainer facilitates the structure of the circle and supports the person in further exploring his or her issue. Because of the nature of the circle, all participants are able to observe the person in the circle; observe the expression of the body as the mind is raising an issue and the body is expressing its reactions to the issue involved. The body is compelled to react. The body inevitably shows its appreciation of the issue. Participants listen to and observe the person in the circle, and they too react to the issue involved. They will notice a reaction that is instantaneous; likeable, unlikeable, or neutral. The circle works as an amplifier of the process of self-exploration. The circle has no beginning and no end as with awareness and this book. It only has a center: awareness.

This book too is an open invitation to self-exploration. You can start reading at any page and whenever you like. You can step in and out of the circle whenever you want. There is only one requirement. As soon as you step into the circle, your self-exploration starts, just like with this book. You can start at any page and allow the hidden awareness in this book to happen. Simply ask yourself while you are reading these words, what you are aware of. What are the sounds around you? What is the posture of your body? Are you aware of your breathing in and breathing out? Can you observe the rising and falling of your thoughts? What are you aware of? This simple question is all it takes to start the process of self-exploration. What are you aware of in this moment? As you will notice, it all starts here.

In this book there is an inevitable element of repetition. The theme awareness will be explored from different angles and perspectives. The message of this book is not to be found in its form, in the exact meaning of the words. Words are used as limited tools to express what is experienced. The issues explored in this book can lead to deepening of insight of awareness. The examples themselves will not provoke this deepening. Just let your own awareness speak with the awareness hidden in this book and awareness will reveal what is of use to you.

In the beginning is awareness.

The story of Cynthia

Cynthia is a young woman in her late twenties. She works as a psychologist. She came to group psychotherapy as part of her training to become a cognitive psychotherapist. The training program consisted of five days in the form of a mindfulness retreat. The circle of awareness is an important part of the program. Formal mindfulness meditation practice is included. On the second day of the program, Cynthia stepped into the circle and stated that she felt very depressed and thought about leaving the program. The other participants were shocked by her disclosure and felt sympathy for her sad mood. Cynthia walked around in the circle, and everyone saw her sad posture. She moved slowly, spoke softly with hanging shoulders and tears in her eyes. Everyone was touched. I validated her depressed feelings warmly by saying that I saw her sad posture and heard what she was saying. I asked Cynthia very gently if she wanted to try an experiment. Cynthia hesitated and then reluctantly agreed to participate. I asked Cynthia to say whatever came into her mind about her depressed mood and while talking, to hop around in the circle. Cynthia looked bewildered and then I asked again in a gentle and compassionate way to explore what will happen. Cynthia started with a few hops while saying that she felt depressed. Then she stopped and explained it didn't work for her. She decided it might be better to just go home. I asked her again in a slightly more insistent way to continue the experiment. Cynthia went on hopping around and explaining how sad she was. Then after a few rounds she started to smile and stated that this was fun for her. The issue she raised seemed to be of less importance. She went on hopping around, and the whole group began supporting her for her bravery in exploring how this might work for her. During the remainder of the training Cynthia stayed in a calm mood with a smile on her face. A few years later when I met her at a conference, she shared her enthusiasm for the experiment and told me how it was a breakthrough in her self-destructive way of thinking about herself.

Circle of awareness

Awareness is the greatest agent for change. (Eckhart Tolle)

The structure of the circle of awareness is as old as humankind. People come together in a circle and share their stories about personal issues, drama, disappointment, and success. Spontaneously and in an open atmosphere, they give feedback. There is a tangible and inspiring energy in the circle. In the circle we observe the wisdom of the body in the moment. We read the body just as it shows itself in the circle. The body clarifies the true story. We observe and listen carefully, there is no room for misunderstanding. The body knows.

The circle is an invitation to self-exploration. The circle follows a number of rules, and a further experience occurs, largely spontaneous, organic, and sometimes almost magic. The trainers provide the necessary security, support, incentive, and encouragement. As a participant you can present whatever has priority for you in this period of your development. You learn to observe yourself in a neutral and accepting way, without judgment. From that self-compassionate stance you can come to the right choices for you. Prior to the circle there is a warm-up in the form of meditation exercises to help you activate an accepting attitude.

The circle in its basic form lets participants explore their bodily sensations, emotions, and cognitions. The training starts with learning to observe bodily sensations in a neutral way. Observing how the breath moves through the body, how the breath moves the nostrils, chest, and belly. We bring our attention to this continuous movement and just observe this movement as it is. Whenever we are distracted by perceptions or thoughts — this will happen all the time — we gently bring our attention back to the movement of the breath in the body. By doing this, we train our attention to develop a neutral attitude to the bodily sensations that accompany the movement of the breath through the body. It is a continuous movement that will stay with us our whole life. The awareness of this movement forms a neutral referential point to return our attention to over and over again. By doing this we develop a neutral and calm state of mind. Our mind calms down and then will be able to sink into this endless state of awareness. There is really nothing special to be done and nothing special to get involved in. Just by noticing the movement of the breath in the body, we gradually become more aware of this always-available neutral and calm state of mind. Then we can apply this neutral attitude to other situations. For instance we can observe how emotions like anger or fear are moving through the body, how fear creates tension in our limbs, raises our heart rate, and makes us sweat.

The circle as a structure is about exploring and exchanging experiences. It is not about exchanging ideas. There is no debate going on in the circle. The circle is an experiential structure. The mind, even though it has its use in daily life, has a secondary role in this game. In the circle we explore the experiences that consciousness has. We use the body as our ultimate reference of reality. The mind is used to having leadership in our life; in the circle we ask the mind to step back and leave the stage to give room to awareness and the body, to allow feelings to float freely and to explore them just as they are – another experience. By disconnecting feelings from stories, we can see what feelings actually induce. Fear induces safety behavior and seeks security. Fear induces catastrophic stories that justify the appearance of fear. And they are stories that will be told over and over again. Fear provokes the mind to make a set of rules that will help to prevent a threatening situation from appearing again. The mind will execute these rules rigorously.

The circle of awareness is like a laboratory. In the circle, we explore issues of participants by inviting them to explore their feelings. We allow feelings to appear in an open and compassionate atmosphere and validate feelings when they appear. An issue is raised and while raising the issue, feelings arise. The body shows the feelings while the person tells about the issue. Thoughts and feelings are connected and cause each other. If there is a strong feeling, a thought will appear to justify the strength of the feeling. Feelings don't just appear. There is always a cause for them. Thought claims to be the cause. In the circle we explore this connection.

Awareness and conditioning

The strengthening of behavior which results from reinforcement is appropriately called conditioning. In operant conditioning we strengthen an operant in the sense of making a response more probable, or in actual fact, more frequent.
(B.F. Skinner)

Things appear in a moment. This moment is all there is. Before anything appears, there is nothing. Things appear in the awareness of this moment. We can't see this moment as such. We can only see what we perceive in this moment. We are only aware of this moment because of the things that appear in this moment. We perceive things and things appear to us as perceptions. If we look carefully we can see that there are no real things as such. All that appears are the perceptions of the so-called things. We perceive visions, smells, textures, sounds, and tastes. And even though things appear as solid forms that can be recognized as the same form over and over again, with the same sensual features, all that we can be aware of are the perceptions of these so-called things. They are the things that appear in a moment, over and over again. We can sit in a chair and watch the table and notice the same table over and over again from moment to moment.

And of course, by the repetition of the perception of the table, we conclude that the same table will appear in a next moment. This kind of knowing is the result of conditioning. We know from our experience that if the conditions do not change, the table will appear in the next moment. The perceptual world outside, the world of things and objects which appear to us as perceptual sensations, is the result of conditioning. We know from our experience that things will appear depending on the circumstances.

What is happening before things appear? Nothing is happening. Before anything can appear there is nothing. Everything appears in this moment and before this moment there is nothing.

Everything that appears, appears in our awareness. Awareness is always there. We are aware of the objects through our perception of the objects as we are aware of our thoughts, images, bodily sensations, and feelings. We are aware of them. It is the same awareness we have of different objects. Awareness is the basis for everything that appears. When we look anywhere, inside or outside, we will find awareness. We are aware of the inside and outside world in a moment, and yet we almost certainly know that, if the circumstances remain the same, the same things will appear in the next moment. Part of our awareness is conditioned. That part structures its content depending on the conditions perceived. It perceives a sequence of incidents and structures a contingency. The conditioned part of our awareness is also known as mind. Mind is a very useful part of our awareness. It helps us, from moment to moment, to find our way through time and space.

We can ask ourselves how this conditioning actually happens? Do we condition ourselves to believe in the appearance of objects like tables and chairs? Do we order the objects to appear out of nothing? Of course this is counterintuitive. The objects are just there and will be there independent from our conditioned mind. The existence of the objects is not the result of conditioning. Objects are not provided by the mind. Only the appearance of the objects can be connected to the mind. And for the mind, this is all there is. Wherever we look we will not find any object as such. We can only be aware of its appearance. The mind has conditioned itself, and by doing so, the mind can predict the occurrence of new events. It is our own awareness that is conditioned so that we can create expectations about a future moment and in that future moment compare the appearance of objects with our expectations.

Our mind is stuck in the moment. Even though we can predict with reasonable certainty the appearance of objects in the future, our expectations or predictions are what exist in this moment. This type of awareness of the moment is time and space limited. By the nature of the conditioning process our momentary awareness is time and space limited. This does not mean that awareness itself is time and space limited. On the contrary, many scholars claim that awareness is unlimited in time and space, and numerous individuals speak of an unlimited state of awareness. Here we explore the nature of the conditioned mind and then maybe the mind will reveal part of its true nature by observing and exploring itself very carefully.

All living creatures adapt to their environment by following their conditioning. Life itself is full of change. In adapting to their environment, living creatures are conditioned and live a more or less predictable life. This process of conditioning is executed automatically. It is happening without the interference of awareness. We don't need consciousness to be conditioned. For instance, if we experience a severe trauma under a specific set of circumstances, even a small part of the original circumstances is enough to relive the traumatic experience. Exposed to some features of traumatic environment, we observe the fearful reactions of the body; muscle tension, fast breathing, sweating, trembling etc. This just happens.

Conditioned awareness is limited by its nature. It can only exist in the moment. By first placing itself in a sequence of events and then reaching out for future events and evaluating the past, the mind is *a fortiori* convinced of the truth of the momentary experience as being the only possible experience. We can fantasize about time travel or non-local connection, but we know from our daily experience that we only live this moment in this specific space. Maybe that's why this conditioned awareness tries to escape the moment by filling itself with thoughts about future and past. Evaluating the past and making plans for the future is how the mind constantly tries to improve. The conditioned awareness, the mind, also known as the separate self, is always busy doing something. The separate self or conditioned awareness, as we state here, is a state of awareness. Awareness in a state of conditioning narrows the perspective of awareness itself and creates an illusion of limitations. If we let go of this narrow perspective, we can experience awareness in its true nature, unlimited in time and space. If we look around from this perspective we will find no boundaries, no beginning, no end, just this experience. We find ourselves in this moment not as a result of searching but as recognition. This recognition is not restricted to this moment and this place, this here and now. This recognition is the revelation that we are always there and will always be there. For us it is unimaginable and unexperiential not to be where we are. Whenever awareness is, we are there. We are always there, independent of the circumstances. The only constant factor is our own presence in time and space. Whatever is happening and appearing is due to conditioning. Nothing can appear to us outside the realm of time and space. The so-called outside world is filled with objects. All objects have features, and conditioning restricts all the appearances of objects. All things appear in this state of conditioned awareness. In this state of conditioned awareness, we know how A and B are connected. If A happens, B will follow. We can predict the occurrence of B by noticing the occurrence of A. In the outside world nothing happens by coincidence. The existence and occurrence of things in time and space are contingent and logically connected. All things influence each other, even if this influence is barely detectable. The conditioned world is logically closed. Everything follows logic. Outside the logical world nothing is possible. Even though we can talk about a square circle, we will not find anything like that in the world.

Here we talk about things with distinguishable features. Things with distinguishable features can be manipulated. From the occurrence of A we can predict the occurrence of B. If B happens, this does not necessarily mean that A has occurred. For instance, if Peter drops a pen to the ground and as a result the pen is lying on the ground, this does not necessarily mean that if a pen is lying on the ground, Peter dropped the pen. Anna could have caused this fact by bumping the table, for example. Different events can cause the same effect. And one event can unchain a cascade of effects. If we look at the conditioned world, we see a well-ordered world with predictable events; a logical world with all kinds of conditioned behaviors; an automated world where everything and every event is logically connected. In such a world, it does not really matter much whether we are aware or not. Everything just happens by itself and for itself.

Function of awareness

To believe that I, awareness, share the limits and the destiny of
the mind and body is like believing that the screen shares the
limits and destiny of a character in a movie. (Rupert Spira)

Awareness is being present with the flow of experiences. Awareness is the room where experiences occur. Awareness is a necessary condition for experiences to occur. While experiences are limited in time and space, awareness is not. We know from our experience that experiences come and go. Around the limited experience is a limitless space that extends the experience itself.

The role of awareness seems to be restricted to comparing expectations of the past with the appearance of events in the moment and making a choice whether to continue or change a certain action. Every event has the basic quality of attractive, neutral, or unattractive. We approach an attractive event, avoid an unattractive one, and continue our action when presented with a neutral event. We don't need to be aware of this tendency. The tendency is already there as a result of conditioning. Conditioned awareness is a sufficient cause for the reaction to take place.

Everything is happening in this moment. This moment is all there is. Yet, if we look for the limits of this moment, we can't find them. We only notice the flow of experiences, how one experience flows into another. In conventional language we speak of a moment, but there is no moment as such to be found in our experience or in our awareness. There is only the here and now experience of this.

We can shape objects into forms that will remain in the future. Daily life is full of actions like this. Our culture is the result of shaping and reshaping objects into forms we can use as instruments for our convenience. Awareness follows this process of shaping and reshaping objects into forms. Awareness follows the stream of changes through time. Awareness is being present, nonjudgmental. Awareness is not to be found in the moment. The moment is in awareness. The moment is not an objective fact as such, limited in time, but a subjective experience of here and now. Awareness is not to be found in an experience. The experience is in awareness. Even though it is the same awareness that is always there independent of the changes in time and space, we know from our experience that things change, as do our feelings, thoughts, and bodily sensations. Change is happening all the time.

Awareness is neutral and does not identify with the objects that appear in awareness. Conditioned awareness, or the thinking mind, thinks that it corresponds with the stream of changes. Conditioned awareness sees itself as a changing object and is looking for constant factors like the shape of a body or traits of the person. Conditioned awareness sees constant factors in things, and by seeing them, concludes that it must find these constant factors in its own realm of experience.

Unconditioned awareness or awareness remains unchanged, un-attached, available for every change.

In daily life, awareness seems to correspond with its contents: thoughts, feeling, and bodily sensations. In exceptional circum-stances, like a near accident, awareness expands in a broader realm than the experience itself. The experience of time and space seems to expand. It is like the individual becomes super conscious. It is these kinds of experiences that show that awareness is broader than the experience.

Awareness of sensations

Do not become a mere recorder of facts, but try to penetrate
the mystery of their origin. (Ivan Pavlov)

Philosophers like Heidegger and Nietzsche say that we are
thrown into this world without the knowledge of what to do and
then discover by trial and error how to adapt to this world. Our
body is reacting all the time to sensations outside or inside the
body. All these sensations develop instantaneously the quality of
attractiveness, unattractiveness, or neutral. What is attractive to
the body will lead to 'approach behavior'. Unattractive will lead to
'escape behavior' and with neutral stimuli, the body will continue
the same pattern of behaviors. This is an automated process of
adaptation and conditioning. Our awareness can seem to be in a
state of sleep; a very useful state that enables us to manage all the
numerous stimuli and sensations that we have to adapt to. And it
seems as if we determine our actions, but actually our actions
happen as a result of our conditioning. The mind, the ego, the
conditioned awareness, all function like a sleeping state. This all
seems very counterintuitive so let's have a closer look at this process.

How do we keep ourselves asleep? And if we do, how can we wake ourselves up? Do we have to analyze our thoughts rigorously and classify our actions as good or bad? Do we have to do anything to wake ourselves up? Logic tells us we have to do something to change the state we are in. Change is the consequence of an action by something or someone. So what can we do to change the state we are in? As sleeping persons, we won't be able to change anything. Conditioned as we are, there is no way we can influence the process. We should not ask how to become awake. That's a paradoxical question. As soon as we consciously change the situation from a sleeping state to awake, this is proof of not being asleep. The same is true for conditioning. As soon as we deliberately change the situation, we step out of the process of conditioning. We should not ask ourselves how to escape the situation but how we keep ourselves stuck in the situation. Let's explore how we keep ourselves asleep. If we look closely at our experiences, we might notice that they come and go. None of them are forever; there is this constant stream of pleasant, unpleasant, and neutral experiences. What we do all the time is approach the pleasant experiences and try to multiply them while escaping and avoiding the unpleasant experiences. This becomes familiar, and we are hardly aware of this very fundamental conditioned process. So let's examine this process, not with the aim to change it, but just to observe it; not on a special occasion, but just in daily life. Let's explore our tendency to approach and avoid. What do we see? Does anyone consciously choose te approach or avoid? Is anyone in charge? Look carefully for that person, that entity. All we see is this tendency emerging in the actual situation and dissolving again. Notice the tendency to attach to pleasant experiences and notice how this tendency moves you. Take for instance your breakfast preference for tea or coffee. Notice how strong this habit of drinking tea or coffee at breakfast is. Don't change it, just observe it. Notice how this tendency organizes your behavior at breakfast. You can see that you have to do something. You have to narrow your focus of attention and perform the coffee or tea drinking ritual. You know from your experience that if you or someone else would obstruct the performance of your breakfast ritual, your mood would change from neutral to unpleasant which is something you want to avoid; so you prefer to execute your habit as you are used to doing. In a way, your breakfast ritual is automated and conditioned. By staying in the state of conditioned awareness, we keep ourselves asleep by clinging to pleasant events and avoiding unpleasant ones. We exclude all other possible experiences of that moment, not by choice but as a result of conditioning. All it takes for conditioning to take over is to have a soft focus on our preferences and allow it to organize our daily lives. When this happens we narrow our focus on our preferences and avoid the possibility of change. Although this kind of attachment is soft and subtle, we know from our experience that changing it can disturb our comfortable mood. Something is causing this daily life process. Even though we cannot say specifically who is responsible for our rituals, we know that we don't want them to be disturbed. In a way we are guarding our rituals or at least something is guarding them. To keep ourselves in this conditioned awareness state, we have to perform a subtle mind shift, a subtle shift in perspective from broad to narrow. So let's step out of this narrow perspective and start observing our tendencies at breakfast. Observe the movements of your body. Observe your bodily sensations, your feelings, and your thoughts while performing your breakfast ritual. Don't change it, just observe it. Stop thinking about how you are performing your breakfast ritual but instead observe how it performs itself. Observe the pattern of conditioning that is performing itself automatically. It is a very subtle change in perspective with a profound possibility for change. This change can happen not by doing something but by stopping seeing yourself as the doer. When this happens the conditions will not change; the same circumstances remain with the same habits, and the same conditioning will occur. The only change is a change of perspective from a conditioned awareness to a state of pure awareness; a mindful state of unconditioned awareness. It is in this state that things are just happening as they happen and where there is no longer an 'I' avoiding things happening or striving for things to happen. It is a state where we allow things to happen and trust them to happen again in their own way.

This is the state we facilitate in the circle of awareness. We know from the hundreds of participants who have visited the circle that one can easily enter this state just by allowing the body to act as it acts.

Awareness of emotions

There is no illusion greater than fear. (Lao Tzu)

Emotions are all about me. It's me experiencing anger, anxiety, and sadness. And it's me who wants to get rid of these overwhelming feelings. Emotions are experienced as disturbances of our quiet mood. We need to act upon the emotions in order to restore our mood. As soon as emotions appear, stories in our head are activated and tell us why we are in this emotional state; because something terrible happened to us, we react emotionally. Because someone did something and threatened our very existence, we have to react emotionally. The stories in our head tend to exaggerate the situation. These stories are far from neutral. They are instead very subjective and tell us how we perceive the world and ourselves. Stories in our head and emotions form a dangerous alliance. They amplify each other, and they confirm and justify their mutual existence. People who are angry are always completely right. A story that is told in an angry mood is a true story. People around the angry person are encouraged to accept the truth of the story. Of course we all know that this is only true for the angry person. The truth of a story is more the result of collecting and comparing reasonable arguments, pro and con, than of the emotional underpinning of that story. Still we can see that we try to convince others over and over by adding emotional expressions to a story. So what are the benefits of this seemingly ineffective and silly system? An emotional state evidently does not lead to truthful insights about ourselves and the world around us. So let's have a look at the benefits of an emotional state.

Whenever we are in an emotional state, change is happening. We try to accomplish change in our outside world, and if this doesn't work, the change happens *to* us. Our convictions about the world and ourselves will then change. Emotions have this adaptive function. The world around us adapts to us, and we adapt to the world. Let's look inside this process of emotional change. We can notice how emotions affect our experience. First we notice a change in our bodily sensations. For instance with anger, we feel tension in our muscles, we notice the sharpening of our senses and preparation for action. The change in our bodily sensations tells us something relevant is happening. We look around, scan our environment. We look for the cause of the change in our mood. We know from previous experience that this kind of change means that something important is about to happen. What we experience is true. The fact of our experience is there. We cannot deny our experience, we cannot deny the change in our bodily sensations. This change in our bodily sensations affects our self-image directly in that moment. It only takes a split second to transform from a neutral self to an emotional self. We experience the bodily change. Simultaneously we perceive our environment and connect the occurrence of this bodily change to the occurrence of stimuli in the environment. Our experience in that moment consists of the perception of bodily sensations and external stimuli. In an emotional state there is no time to contemplate what's happening. It all goes too fast. In the same moment a memory is constructed. The memory is a reduction of the current numerous stimuli and sensations in that moment. The story that evolves is a meaningful explanation for the event and is added to the pattern of stimuli and bodily sensations. The event that affected our emotional mood becomes part of our autobiographical memory. This memory acts as a useful template for recognition of comparable future events and activates proper behavior in that moment. The next time, we will only need a small set of stimuli to activate the memory and prepare us for the possibility of a repeat of the disturbing situation and then activate the right action. This is a process we know as conditioning. Emotions condition us to the world around us. They help us form vast convictions about ourselves and the world around us. Emotional changes happen so fast that we are hardly aware of what is happening or the conditioning that takes place.

Before reason there is emotion. The simple fact that a meaningful change has taken place implies an emotional reaction. Why is it that emotions play such a crucial role in our lives? Emotions have this adaptive function that helps us move through the world. Emotions, like other events, are labeled as a like or dislike. By nature emotions are not neutral. Emotions affect us. If we like an emotion we want more of it, and we want to experience this emotion over and over. We get attached to an emotional state in the same way that we get attached to objects. As a matter of fact, emotion is what creates attachment. Whatever we are attached to has an emotional meaning for us. And if an emotional event is happening, it is always meaningful as well. In daily life we wonder and often ask each other why the emotion is there. This daily practice suggests that emotion has a reason to come to the fore. It seems there are no emotions without a reason. When a little child comes home crying, the mother will ask what has happened to the child that caused the tears to appear? When the child tells the story, the mother will judge whether or not the emotion is reasonable. While growing up, we learn that emotions occur for a reason. So it seems that emotions need a reason to exist.

Let's have a look at daily life and see whether this is true. You walk down the street. You are in a bit of a hurry because you want to be on time for an appointment. Someone approaches you and asks if he can speak with you. Without waiting for your reply, he starts selling his product, a local paper. You notice some irritation in yourself and decide to move on. Situations like this are a part of daily street life in the city. In this sequence of events, it all starts with you being goal-directed and in a hurry. You are at ease with what you are doing. Nothing really strange or special is happening. It is just you moving down the street, in a bit of a hurry. Then this person approaches you. A new situation develops and presents you with a challenge about how to adapt. You expected to move on to your appointment, but this expectation proved to be wrong. Someone interfered with it. It is relatively of no great importance. It is just you wanting to move on and someone distracting you from your aim. You are in a slightly alert state because you are in a little bit of a hurry. The incident is not neutral for you. The incident is instantaneously labeled as unattractive. This isn't because someone is seeking your attention for what he considers to be a profitable deal for both of you, and it's not solely because you are in hurry. The qualification of the situation is a result of the interaction of these two factors. Your being in a hurry and the person seeking your attention are both in themselves neutral events. The place where they come together is where the emotional reaction occurs. So you walk along, in a bit of a hurry, and someone approaches you and you want to move on. You notice that you dislike the approach of the other person. Dislike is just there. The simple registering of dislike could help you stick to your own goal and walk on. But instead of noticing and validating your dislike, you stood still and got involved in a commercial conversation. Irritation emerges and you start to explain to the other person that he should stop bothering you and you need to move on. Your emotional reaction follows the disregarding of your own registering of dislike. First there is the signal of dislike, then the emotional reaction, and then the explanation. Your emotional reaction is meant to help you stick to your own path or to help you adapt to the new situation and explore what opportunities this new situation offers you. Your dislike of the interference by the salesman on the street is not a necessary result of the interference. Dislike is an effect of the interaction. Dislike is the first signal. If you notice and validate your dislike, it's easy to say no and move on. The emotional reaction is no longer necessary and does not arise. And maybe you will even feel slightly more confident and comfortable because you were able to move on and follow your own course.

Emotions tell us that something of importance is going on and that we should pay attention to it and evoke suitable change. When we ignore or neglect this appeal, the emotion will become stronger and more energy will be directed to the environment or towards ourselves. Change has to come in us or in the environment. We have to adapt. The perception of like or dislike is there and immediately the tendency to approach or escape appears. What comes first in this process? If we look at our experience, dislike or like is there and from that evolves the tendency to approach or escape. We notice like or dislike, but how do we notice them? We notice the tendency and experience like or dislike. We notice an energy floating through our body, and this energy results in approach or avoidance behavior. Just like a flavor we taste, or a sound we hear, a smell we smell, we instantaneously experience like, dislike, or neutral. Before the tendency of approach or avoidance is there, the perception of like, dislike, or neutral is there. If we look carefully at what happens before the emotion arises, we notice the perception of like or dislike. After that a chain of reactions follows. Like or dislike will automatically evoke approach or avoidance behavior. We bring our attention to this new object and explore its features with our senses, or we pull our attention away from this object and try to ignore it. We move our body toward this new object, maybe grasp it, hold it, and explore the likeness of this object, or we move away from it and confirm the dislike of the object and go to a neutral state again. If we move toward the liked object and the attractiveness of the object is confirmed again, we will experience a pleasant emotion and get attached to the object that caused these pleasant feelings. Or if we try to move away from the disliked object but we are not able to escape from it, we will get frustrated and experience anger and maybe try to chase the object away. Emotions create change in our connections with the world around us. Emotions are useful for the adaptive process, an adaptive process that starts with the perception of likes and dislikes. The confirmation of likes and dislikes follows. The last step is formed by the stories that arise. We like to tell each other and our self about our emotional events. We share our stories and by doing so confirm our emotional reactions. We undergo an adaptive process and as a result stories appear and are shared. We share a world and common values. By telling our stories we confirm our mutual values and sense of community. Emotional stories have a binding quality.

Here is an example. You share a desk with a colleague at the office. Your colleague puts some personal items on the desk. You notice an irritation in yourself, and you decide not to share this with your colleague. When you get home, you share your opinion about this colleague with your partner. You describe your colleague as an egocentric character who doesn't consider others. Your partner supports you, and you both conclude that it is hard to collaborate with such an egocentric colleague. As a result of your adaptive emotional process, the opinion about your colleague has changed and you and your partner are both convinced of the truth of your opinion about this colleague. The outcome of your adaptive emotional process is this change in your opinion about this colleague. Your partner validates this opinion. You and your partner are now more aware of the common values you share. Living in this world means sharing time and space with other human beings, and inevitably we can get involved in a conflict of interest about time and space with other people around us. Emotion starts whenever something of importance is at stake. Whenever a meaningful event occurs that touches our interest in things or people we are attached to, emotion will follow. The next time that even a small aspect of that situation appears again, the whole emotional program will start over. In this way the same story will be confirmed and the same behavioral pattern will be executed. The next time someone refers to this story or conviction, the emotion will arise again and you will anticipate the occurrence of the same event.

The story and the behavioral pattern are conditioned and will automatically arise if referred to or if confronted with a set of eliciting stimuli.

Awareness of thoughts

Observe the space between your thoughts, then observe the observer. (Hamilton Boudreaux)

What a smell is for the nose, a thought is for thinking. As the body reacts to a smell, the body reacts to a thought. For the body, thought and smell are just stimuli. And all stimuli have an instantaneous effect — the appreciation of attractive or unattractive. In the case of an attractive stimulus, the body will try to approach the stimulus. In the case of an unattractive stimulus, the body will try to escape. In other words, the body is attracted to pleasant stimuli and will avoid harmful stimuli. This happens automatically all the time and there is no need for awareness to be involved.

The same is true for thoughts. Instantaneous thoughts will be experienced as attractive or unattractive, pleasant or unpleasant. Only the body can't escape from thoughts, just as the body can't approach the thoughts. Thoughts happen in the body as a very intimate experience. Whether pleasant or unpleasant the thoughts are just there, and the body can't escape. But still the body is condemned to react. When approach and escape aren't possible, another response has to occur. In the case of an unpleasant thought, the body will react with a freezing response. The freezing response, in this case, is not anticipatory of the well-known fight or flight response but is just the only response that is left. The body reacts by freezing at unpleasant and harmful thoughts. The mind will notice the unpleasantness in the body and interpret this as proof of the correctness of the thought. For instance, thinking about an unpleasant colleague gives an unpleasant feeling in the body and this unpleasant feeling is considered to be proof of the unpleasantness of the colleague. Let's assume this is true. This does not mean that if you think about yourself and you get an unpleasant feeling in your body that this proves that you are indeed an unpleasant person. The response of the body is just a response to the thought. It is just a thought your body reacts to, as to a smell, a sound, or whatever sensation is entering your awareness. If there is a pleasant thought in your mind, the body can't approach the thought any more closely. The thought is already as close and intimate as possible. Still the body does react. Pleasant thoughts create more energy. This is easily demonstrated when you are performing an energetic task like jogging. After a few miles, maybe at the end of your planned run through the park, you think about a person you love. You repeat the name of that person in your mind and notice the effect on your body. From my own experience, I know that just the thought of my loved one gave me more energy, more than I normally had at that point on the run. Funnily enough, the mate I was running with was astonished and asked me how it was possible that I had this unusual energy at the end of the run. Normally my mate would be running faster than I at that point. One might explain this as 'good thoughts unblock energy pathways and bad thoughts block energy pathways in the body.' I invite you to investigate this for yourself. Truly a funny experiment with your thoughts.

Many thoughts are just neutral. The body does not react to them. The body just keeps on doing what it is doing, as it does with other neutral stimuli. The body won't react to them. If a neutral sound comes to your ear or a neutral smell enters your nose, you won't react. There is no tendency to approache, escape, or freeze. The disturbance of this neutral state is what activates your attention and awareness. This disturbance will be noticed and instantly experienced as attractive or unattractive. It is here that we can investigate the impact of thoughts. Neutral thoughts have no specific meaning and can be thought without disturbance. One might say that these thoughts fit you well. Disturbing thoughts in a way don't fit. Disturbing thoughts will cause an effect. From the effect, we can learn something about the usefulness of these thoughts. Negative, catastrophic thoughts will have an unpleasant disturbance in the body. From this reaction, you know whether or not the thought fits the body. It is very useful to ask yourself how it is for your body to notice the appearance of a specific thought.

You are not your thoughts. As you are not the smell in your nose, the sound in your ears, the vision in your eyes, the taste in your mouth, the touch on your skin. You are not your thoughts. Thoughts will tell you that it is you who is thinking your thoughts as it is you who is smelling the smell. Let's assume this is true. But should the conclusion then be that you are the smell in your nose? Of course not. Thoughts come and go. You don't know where they come from and you don't know where they will go. They just come and go. The mere fact that you are thinking your thoughts is no proof of your existence. As the mere fact that you are smelling these smells is no proof of your existence.

Thinking is doing, to be is to be; you don't have to think to be, you have to be to think.

Thoughts are very useful for solving a problem or planning an action. Our whole culture and design of our society are the result of thinking. With our thoughts, we can design numerous things and construct them later in the outside world. As we know, the design of a building is not the same as the building itself. The same is true for thoughts. Thoughts refer to and represent objects in the outside world; these references or representations are not the same as the objects themselves.

Thoughts are bound to logic. It is, for instance, impossible to try not to think. You cannot not think. There is no way of doing that, just as there is no way of stopping your thinking. As long as you try to stop your thinking, you will keep on thinking. But we can learn from experience that there is an empty space between thoughts. A space you can become aware of by giving thought an impossible instruction, for instance to try not to think of a specific object. Then the object will appear in your thoughts. As a next step, you instruct yourself to think neutral or empty your mind and if the thought of the object reappears, to welcome the thought. I have practiced this exercise with many participants, and a lot of them experienced the empty space between thoughts. Another impossible instruction is to observe the beginning of a thought. Since that is impossible, the mind will stop thinking for a moment. You can also ask yourself to think of a square circle. You will learn that you can think the words but not the square circle. Another reason for the mind to give up for a moment.

Roughly we can distinguish two kinds of thinking processes, analytic thinking and synthetic thinking. Analytic thinking focuses on definitions, equations, comparisons, systematically investigating a problem. No new information is added, the solution is to be found in what is known already. Synthetic thinking, on the other hand, focuses on integrating new facts into the trusted knowledge. Synthetic thinking is open to new facts. Analytic thinking is closed to new facts. Analytic thinking rearranges known facts or insights and by doing so can create new insight. While integrating new facts, synthetic thinking creates new insight.

In daily life analytic thinking can easily result in ruminating, rethinking a problem over and over without finding any new solutions. Thinking itself won't stop this ruminating; as long as the thinking is there, a new solution seems possible. Thinking is the domain of the mind. Without thinking, it seems that the mind stops existing. Even though there is no real need to think things over and over, the mind will continue doing so as a reason for existence. The mind will try to avoid the empty space between thoughts. The mind can't find any mind in that place, a state of no-mind. From the perspective of the mind, it is completely understandable that the mind is not attracted to a state of no-mind. Still, without doubt, meditation practitioners experience the empty space between thoughts. The mind needs its synthetic capability in order to contemplate this new fact. The logical conclusion seems to be that, given the truth of an emptiness between thoughts, thoughts are not necessary conditions for existence. The argumentation 'I think, therefore I am' is false. Thinking is overrated. The argumentation should be: 'I am, and I think.' While noticing that I am, being aware of my existence, I can be aware of numerous things and processes. Thinking is just one of those processes.

Transforming quality of awareness

Anna is a woman in her mid-forties. She came to a mindfulness retreat as part of her meditation practice. The circle was part of the program. Anna was excited by the method of the circle and kept telling everyone how good the trainer had been at his job as well as how nice it had been for her when she finally understood the process of insight mediation. Every time another participant stepped into the circle to explore his or her issues, Anna was eager to give her feedback about the psychological background of the issue raised. Finally she stepped into the circle herself and wanted to explore her own feelings of inferiority. I started by suggesting to her how she might explore her feelings of inferiority by observing the way she moved her body. Anna adapted to this suggestion by taking a humble posture, walking around and expressing what came to her mind. At my suggestion she chose a participant member of the group by whom her feelings of inferiority were activated, and explored what kinds of thoughts came to her mind and observed the chain of emotions that developed while doing this. Anna worked hard. She was able to express her thoughts, and while doing so explain them to the trainers. She replied that this was all very helpful in understanding her feelings of inferiority. Still, even though Anna stated that she understood it much better, her body showed no relief. She kept walking with her head bent low and shoulders tensed. When I shared this observation, she was surprised and confused. She tried to correct her posture, and a painful expression came to her face. I suggested to her that she keep observing this pain and accept it as a gift. Anna agreed and sat down in the circle. At the end of the group session that morning, while I made some final remarks about the remainder of the program, Anna started to cry and said that it hurt very much. I asked her to stay while the rest of the group went for lunch. Sitting together, I asked Anna to observe the pain and keep her focus on the pain by just observing the pain here and now. We both sat there for about half an hour and remained fully aware of the pain. Anna kept on saying how much it hurt, and I supported her by inviting her to stay in the moment and allow the pain to be just as it is. In this state of full presence and awareness, a shift occurred. The pain dissolved completely and Anna became fully aware and clear minded. This state remained for the rest of the day, and later Anna described this as a real breakthrough and relief of her suffering from an abused childhood.

Conditioned mind

All conditioning aims at that: making people like their
inescapable social destiny. (Aldous Huxley)

The conditioned mind is not able to observe anything other than its own routine and habits. If a problem is raised, the mind wants to solve it in a routine way. We need awareness in order to step out of the routine of the mind. By observing what is happening from moment to moment in a neutral way, we open up to new aspects of our environment and ourselves. The conditioned mind tells us stories about who we are, how we should evaluate ourselves and the world around us. The conditioned mind is convinced of the truth of the stories it tells itself. The conditioned mind is not aiming for new insights; it seeks confirmation of old ones. It reconstructs the same convictions over and over. It tries to tell us the story of who we really are. When we wake up in the morning we find the same self with the same convictions and then we confirm them over and over again through the day. Habits by nature are not open to change. We know from our experience how hard it is to change convictions about ourselves and the world around us. Yet change is happening all the time.

The conditioned mind is filled with thoughts, fear, and ambition resulting in a firm competitive stance, a stance that was useful in the early days of humankind but that nowadays seems to stand in the way of real progress. The conditioned mind aims to maintain who or what you are, an automatic process that is hard to change. A way to change our convictions is by consciously testing these convictions in real life. For instance, if you think of yourself as a complete failure, you can look for proof to discount this thought. Cognitive psychotherapy is all about testing so-called dysfunctional beliefs about yourself and the world in 'behavioral experiments'. For instance if you think people will disapprove of a certain behavior of yours, you can test this by asking people about this directly. Dysfunctional emotions like social fear are caused by dysfunctional thoughts about others and ourselves. A socially phobic person is convinced that others will disapprove of him or her and will avoid social encounters with others or will seek approval from others all the time as a compensation for the risk of disapproval. Social phobics lack a quality of self-validation and are dependent on other-validation. Social phobia is a common fear in our society, and many people suffer from this fear in one way or another. By avoiding social encounters or thinking negatively of themselves while presenting themselves to others, the habit of negative self-evaluation is rewarded and gets stronger. As a result it feels more comfortable to keep avoiding social encounters rather than to confront themselves with the possibility of disapproval or rejection by others.

Therapeutic use of awareness

Everything you want is on the other side of fear. (Jack Canfield)

An effective way to learn to swim is to start by getting yourself in the water. You can only learn to swim by getting wet. The same is true for social fear. If you want to learn to cope with social fear, you have to put yourself into situations where the fear of rejection or disapproval could be triggered.

Herman was a young man in his late twenties. He participated in a training group for mindfulness where participants learn to cope with social and intimacy issues. Herman was fearful of rejection by attractive women and didn't dare talk to them. He stepped into the circle with this issue, stating that he loved women but was not able to approach them. He felt ignored by women and on the few occasions he did dare to approach them, he was rejected. I started by validating his fear and introduced myself as an experienced collector of rejections from attractive women. I invited Herman to join in a rejection experiment by approaching the attractive women in the circle and disclosing his fear of rejection to them. The circle consisted of approximately twenty-five participants with several very attractive women among them. I asked Herman if I could support him while he approached one of these attractive women and disclosed to her his fear of rejection by her. I stood right beside Herman while he *was saying these fearful words. Then as soon as Herman finished his phrase, I took Herman to the center of the circle and asked him how this experiment was for him. Herman evaluated it as very frightening and hard to do. His body trembled with fear. I took Herman to another woman with the same procedure and repeated this several times. Herman started to feel more confident, and at the end of this series of experiments a self-confident Herman was talking to an attractive woman about his fear of rejection but he was now able to handle it. A warm and enthusiastic round of applause from the group was the spontaneous reward for Herman.*

The mind is like a house rebuilding and reconstructing itself in an apparently solid structure. The mind is telling the story of how things are or should be and is always commenting on itself and the world. And by commenting, it polishes the self to an apparently solid form. The mind consists of stories about ourselves and the world we live in. The self as a construct in the middle of the mind is like a narrative at the center of gravity. It appears to have a sustainable form, but in the course of time, it is reconstructed so it can easily fit with the biography of the person involved. As with everything in this world, the mind is subject to change.

We know from experience that change is happening, but what is causing this change? The world is always changing, we are adapting to this changing world all the time, and all the wile the self shows itself as a solid structure. This process of adaptation is accompanied by friction and tension. The self strives towards a solid form in a changing environment. This is where we need emotions. Emotions help the mind to adapt effectively to the changes in the world. Emotions by their nature create motion in the self and in the environment. Emotions evoke motion.

Emotions turn the self inward or outward. Emotions are constructive or destructive for objects in or outside; for example, joy is an
outward and constructive emotion and despair, on the other hand,
is inward and destructive. Anger is outward and destructive. And
ineffective anger or dysfunctional anger will transform into depression, which is an inward and destructive emotion.

Transforming pain

The cure for pain is in the pain. (Rumi)

Emotions need to be validated in order to become effective. If emotions are ignored by the self or significant others, the emotions will become dysfunctional and destructive. Emotions in their true nature are a form of energy that can help the individual adapt to changing circumstances. If not used in a proper way, emotions as living force can transform into a self-destructive energy form and cause a lot of suffering. For instance if sadness is not acknowledged or validated by the individual, it will transform into despair and end as chronic pain. The story of Elisa helps us to understand how this process functions.

Elisa is a woman in her late fifties. She came to a five-day workshop for mindfulness training where the circle of awareness forms an important part of the program. When she was in her twenties, Elisa was a professional dancer. Now later in life she suffers from serious backaches and avoids more pain by limiting her movements. Where Elisa moved elegantly and smoothly in her dancing days, she moves awkwardly and restrainedly in her late fifties. In the circle Elisa told the story of her suffering from back pain while her movements were uneasy and cautious. I told her that I saw her cautious movement, and I validated her pain. I was aware that change could only come if Elisa could accept things as they are and see how they affect her life. If Elisa could accept responsibility for this chain of events, she could allow beneficial change to happen. Even though this seems paradoxical, it has been demonstrated on numerous occasions in the circle, and as a trainer I was aware of this. So by validating her pain I facilitated the possibility of beneficial change provided that Elisa accepted the pain as her own pain. I then asked Elisa whether she would participate in an experiment for more acceptance. I asked Elisa whether she could dance with the pain, like the pain was her dance partner. Elisa did, and we could see that she was indeed a professional dancer who still knew how to move her body even when she was in pain. But she moved cautiously and with restraint, and it looked like her energy was still blocked somewhere in her body. After receiving this feedback Elisa recognized her restrained state and confirmed that this was what the pain allowed her to do. She could dance with the pain even though she hated it. Then I asked her if she could change her attitude towards the pain, not dancing with the pain as an alienated object but embracing the pain and dancing from the center of her pain as an intimately felt experience, to listen to what was happening inside and dance from this. A strange thing happened. Elisa stood still, focused on her body, waiting for her inner conductor. Then she started to move, tears streaming down her face. The group silently watched her dance and was touched by the elegant and profound way she moved now. Her movements became smooth and elegant, and the energy of the pain was released and available to her dancing body.

Undoing the doing

The human body is the best picture of the human soul.
(Ludwig Wittgenstein)

The world is as we perceive it. We have no direct knowledge of the world as such. Things are just as they are. How we perceive them is the result of conditioning. The same is true for how we perceive others. We perceive others not as they truly are but through a veil of conditioning. Our opinion of the other, how intimate she or he is, is the result of conditioning. Opinions as such, judgments we have of others and ourselves, emerge during the inevitable process of conditioning. They can occur instantaneously or after a long period of experiencing the other. If an opinion is formed in the mind, the body will react to it with appreciation or aversion. The body can't do anything else. The body always reacts to stimuli with like, dislike, or neutrality. It always reacts with approach or escape. And if the stimulus is neutral, it just goes on with what it was doing. It has no choice. The like, dislike, or neutral reaction is there before consciousness is involved. The start of approach and avoidance behavior is a conditioned response of the body. This is the default state of the body-mind collaboration — perceive stimuli and react to them. Before we are aware of an actual event and how we react to it, our reaction is already there and launches a chain of functional or dysfunctional behaviors. Opinions as well as feelings are the result of conditioning. We cannot and should not blame ourselves for this automatic process. It is just as it happens.

During our process of adaptation to the world around us and during socializing with important others and the society we live in, we are inevitably conditioned. We perceive and react to the world as a result of conditioning. The only domain this conditioning process cannot touch is our consciousness; the awareness of our presence here and now. In order to break through the chains of conditioning, we need to become aware of what is happening in our thoughts, feelings, and bodily sensations and not whether we like or dislike them but learn to observe them as they are. By doing this, a profound change in perspective can happen. Instead of identifying ourselves as a conglomeration of thoughts, feelings, and bodily sensations, we can learn to perceive them as bygones and experiences that come and go. In doing so, the experiences are experienced as they are and no longer constitute our self or so-called true nature. The self is not a composed something that can be reduced to something else.

A moment is just as it is. In the moment there is nothing that needs to go or nothing that needs to stay. By allowing the stream of experiences to happen, we experience freedom in its true nature, not by making our own choices and getting attached to them, not by getting attached to our experiences and pursuing them over and over, but by allowing them to happen in the moment. In taking this stance, our consciousness, our awareness of the present here and now, will expand to timeless space. Poets, mystics, and spiritual teachers talk about this, a state of true intimate awareness of our own being.

It is in this state that we can meet an intimate other. In this intimate encounter there are no boundaries between you and me, there is only this experience of absolute vulnerability and openness to the other and the world around us. The mind is no longer interfering with the experience, is no longer commenting on the experience or trying to improve it, there is just the experience and we are floating on the stream of experiences. You and I dissolve in us. There is only the experience of us; an inter-subjective experience without a subjective self to constitute it. As soon as we try to grab the special features of this state, we fall out of it. It is just experience experiencing experience. It is consciousness being aware of consciousness, experiencing the oneness of all. Is this a special state? No, it is not. It is a state of unconditioned awareness and total presence. Does this state have to last forever? It can but will not. Eventually conditioning takes over, and the routine of daily life will ask our attention for bodily care, household and social issues. Is that a problem? No, it is not. For consciousness there are no problems to be solved. They don't exist. Problems exist only in the mind. The mind deals with problems by noticing them, analyzing and evaluating them, and trying to change the circumstances. For consciousness there are no problems. Consciousness can only observe what happens and by doing so become aware of experiences as they are. By allowing experiences to happen in a compassionate way, experiences will dissolve again and other experiences occur. The mind is in a doing mode, reaching out for something to happen. If we undo the mind from doing, we allow awareness to be just as it is. Awareness is in the being mode, allowing experiences to be experienced.

Illusionary self

The greatest con, that he ever pulled, was making you believe,
that he is you. ("Avi" in *Revolver*)

Look behind doors, look behind curtains, and everywhere you
look, you'll find the same one, always there, you watching you.

The mind does not like to show itself. It hides behind a façade of
conditioned opinions, behaviors, and feelings. If we look behind
this façade there is nothing to be found. Noticing this nothing-
ness is an overwhelming experience and can raise a lot of fear of
losing the illusion of a separate and unique self. Everything that
exists wants to survive. It is the same with the mind. It wants to
subsist. The mind is composed of the lessons we learn from our
experiences with the only purpose of surviving the circumstances where threats have appeared in the past. In order to survive,
the mind exaggerates the anticipated danger of situations and
warns us by telling stories to itself and others about the threats
that might appear. Ultimately the basic feeling of the mind is
anxiety; fear of losing and fear of disappearing. Of course the
mind does not want to reveal this fear. In revealing the fear, the
mind contradicts the illusion of a solid self. The mind hides be-

hind a socially acceptable façade of stories about what might happen and how to deal with it. If we discuss and approach this façade, defenses appear. The mind does not want its true nature of fear and shame to be exposed. The mind needs to be in control of the situation and take precautionary measures so that nothing will damage the illusionary self-image of the mind.

A young man named Adam, who came to an open mindfulness group, illustrates this process. Fifteen people formed the group that evening. It was the first time Adam had joined the group. The evening started as usual with an explanation of the structure of the circle and the aim of self-exploration in the circle. From the beginning Adam wanted to discuss several issues with the trainer. After finishing the introduction, I declared the circle open and allowed the process to start. Adam was the first person to step into the circle, stating that he did not have a special issue but just wanted to experience the circle. I started to work with Adam by asking him whether he was aware of his body and the movements of his body, and I invited Adam to explore his observations. Adam opposed these instructions and wanted to continue his debate, stating that the trainer knew him as Adam from other occasions and that he did not want to collaborate with the structure of the circle as proposed by the trainer. Reluctantly he followed some instructions from me and then he began opposing again. These reactions of Adam were a typical defense of the mind when it feels itself under attack. Even the friendly invitation for self-exploration triggered a tremendous fear. This type of fear does not want to be exposed or experienced; on the contrary, it tries to take control of the situation. Finally Adam gave up and stated he did not want to cooperate anymore. The structure of the circle allows other participants to give feedback to the person who has stepped into the circle. The feedback is given from a third person's perspective. The person is not addressed directly, in order to maintain an observational stance that is so important for gaining insight into the process of self-exploration. Adam received feedback that members of the group felt disturbed and annoyed. Some others suggested that Adam was afraid of showing and exploring himself. After hearing that,

Adam left the room, disqualifying the circle and the members of the group.

Of course there is nothing wrong with Adam's behavior. The circle invites us to explore whatever there is at that moment. Participants are free to explore whatever they want to and decide for themselves how far the exploration can go. The trainer takes care of the safety and integrity of the person involved and of the members of the group, but still this process of self-exploration can be very threatening for the self-image of the person involved. We need a compassionate trainer and group to facilitate this process. Whoever steps into the circle is not to be judged by what he or she shows but is invited to take responsibility for his or her process of self-exploration.

Fear of losing control

Consciousness cannot be known by the mind. The mind is an
object. It does not know anything. It is itself known by
consciousness. (Rupert Spira)

The mind does not want to explore. The mind wants to continue
its task of survival. When fear appears, it's a sign that the mind is
losing its control, its grip on the situation. Only then is there an
opportunity to explore the true nature of fear, to look into the
heart of fear and look the tiger in the mouth, and finally to notice
that there is nothing to be afraid of and nothing to be ashamed of.

If fear appears, it needs to be noticed and validated as fear. Fear
seeks a story to validate its existence. But fear does not need a reason to exist. Out of habit we explain our fear by telling a story that
seemingly caused fear to appear. The story is a sufficient but unnecessary condition for fear to exist. As soon as the fear is present, it does not need a specific story any more. Fear can ask the
mind to create numerous stories that explain the existence of fear
in a particular moment. The mind will create stories that fit per-
fectly with the fear that is being experienced. Feelings and stories
are automatically connected through the mind. Both will subsist
and be experienced as true phenomena by the individual. The

more intense the feeling, the more true the story and vice versa; the more convinced we are of the story, the stronger the feeling. The awareness of the body in that moment evaporates. The only truth is the combination of stories and feelings.

> *An extreme illustration of how this process works can be seen in the case of cardio-phobia. People suffering from cardiophobia are in constant fear of having a heart attack. They cope with that fear by frequently checking their heartbeat. At night while lying in bed, they listen to their heartbeat and notice irregularities. The thought inevitably arises that something terribly wrong is about to happen, like a heart attack. This fear arises and gets stronger and turns into panic. A grievous vi-cious circle of catastrophic thoughts followed by stress reactions evolves from which it is hard to escape. Innocent bodily reactions are interpreted as dangerous events, and as the panic gets stronger, the body responds with even more stress re-actions. This is a very uncomfortable anxiety that results in serious loss of quality of life.*

Anxiety needs to be noticed, recognized, and validated to allow change to happen. The recognition needs to be specifically of the feeling of anxiety itself and not of the story that wants to be told. In a way, the story does not matter and is no longer important. As soon as there is fear, it is a true fact and needs to be recognized as such by the individual. Fear is happening. The story just an-nounced it, and now fear is on the stage asking for all our atten-tion. Just by allowing fear to appear, it will disappear. By denying the existence of fear, it becomes stronger. In a way the story de-nies the existence of fear by claiming all the attention it can get. The stage is crowded with stories, and fear gets a minor role. There is a competition between the storytelling and the experi-encing; in the moment, experience is what we know, so the com-petition should be settled in favor of fear. We thank the story for the announcement of fear and focus our full attention on fear, exposing ourselves to it, observing where in the body fear appears. Is it a warm or a cold sensation? Does it tingle? Is the heart beating faster? We keep on observing fear as it shows itself, and we see that the experience of fear comes and goes.

In observing fear, you can ask yourself how big the fear is. Is it bigger than your body? Is the fear bigger than the room or the house you are in? Or is it even bigger than the town you are in at that moment. By asking yourself these almost childish questions, you will notice that fear has properties. All objects have properties, and all objects can be manipulated. As soon as fear has properties, it can be manipulated.

The mind will tell us that fear will come back, not by itself in a direct way but because of the truth of the mind's catastrophic story. The mind will forecast that catastrophes will happen again, and this allows fear to reappear, underlining the truth of the forecast of the mind. In this phase we need to observe the mind and the body. The mind is telling a story and the body reacts with fear. The story of the mind is made up of a collection of thoughts. Thoughts come and go. Just as fear is a collection of bodily sensations presented together and recognized as fear, the catastrophic story of the mind is also just a collection of convictions and thoughts presented together as another fearful story. And if we look carefully, we can see that thoughts come from nothing and go to nothing. The mind tries to tell us that, because of the intensity of the fear, the thoughts the story is composed of must be true. The mind replaces the factual experience of bodily sensations with the illusionary experience of thoughts. By focusing on the experience of fear, we can accept fear as it is — just a conglomerate of bodily sensations that go by. And by observing the sensations carefully, we see them come and go and the mind becomes quiet again.

Panic and awareness

To escape fear, you have to go through it, not around. (Richie Norton)

Anxiety is prominent in cardiac patients. There are serious reasons for this anxiety. A cardiac attack is indeed a life-threatening incident. Heart failure is also a life-threatening disease. The cardiac patient's mind produces justified stories about the risk of another incident. Even if there are no actual symptoms of another attack, the cardiac patient's mind will create an alert state and notice every disturbance in bodily sensations. Even bodily cues that were previously interpreted as harmless bodily cues are now interpreted as cues for cardiac incidents to appear. Despite frequent visits to the familiy doctor or the emergency room, the fear remains. Those visits give only a brief state of relief from the fear for a short period of time. A vicious cycle of internal bodily cues and catastrophic misinterpretations of these cues arises, and the fear gets stronger, with the impact of serious loss of quality of life. If the mind is confronted with danger, it will shift into the control mode immediately and start searching for warning signs in or outside of the body. As compensation for fear, the mind will seek reassurance. The cardiac patient's mind acts in an even more urgent way, checking heart rhythm, blood pressure, pain signals, and by seeking medical reassurance.

Participants in the mindfulness training group for cardiac patients learn to observe their bodily sensations, emotions, and thoughts in a neutral and accepting way. In the first session participants learn to observe the movement of the breath in their body and how the breath moves the nostrils, chest, and belly. They are advised to observe the movement just as it appears and not to change it in any way. Just observe it as it is. Sometimes this is really hard to do, like when breath itself is sensitized as a frightening sensation. In this sensitized state, bringing your attention to the movement of the breath is far from neutral. Tension arises and hyperventilation can easily occur. Still the instruction remains to just observe how the breathing is happening. Often this is demonstrated when one of the participants develops this stress reaction during the session. When that happens, I ask the participant to observe the movement of the chest, notice the stress and pain in the chest, notice the fast rhythm of the breath and the quickening of the heartbeat. The participant should focus on this and accept that it doesn't have to go and nor does it have to stay. With this accepting attitude, the mind calms down and the fearful state is transformed into a calm state. The chest relaxes and the breath calms down. Participants are always eager to observe this. After such an event they become even more convinced of the benefit of the mindfulness approach for coping with stress. Just observe and you will calm down. Another way to get this calming effect is by shifting your attention from the frightening experience of pain and stress in the chest to a neutral part of your body, for instance the soles of your feet. Observe how your soles touch the ground and focus your attention on the soles of your feet. Notice how this change in focus affects your emotional state. By observing the neutral feet, your awareness will be filled with neutral experiences. Your body will react to that by developing a calm state.

> Corina was a woman in her mid-fifties. She joined the group after a heart attack and an angioplasty. In the group session we talked about this shift of attention from chest to feet. One day she visited a large fair in the city she lived in. Together with her husband, she sat down in one of the exciting attractions. Once the door was closed, she suddenly began to panic. As she started to hyperventilate, her husband noticed the panic and began banging on the door to get it open and then he heard Corina saying out loud, 'Feel your feet on the ground, feel your feet on the ground.' Corina repeated these words several times and calmed down. Her husband was amazed how quickly the panic dissolved and Corina came into a calm state. They stayed in the attraction and enjoyed the excitement. The last session of the group training is with partners. They both proudly told this story and gave an inspirational and encouraging example for the rest of the group about how to cope with fear.

Anxiety and neutrality are not compatible, they exclude each other. A shift of attention from anxiety to neutrality is what matters, and this can bring a calming and beneficial change. If we add awareness to cardiac fears, we will notice the difference between harmful and harmless bodily sensations. From this mindful state one can decide where to focus the attention and if there is something urgent to be done.

One makes free-floating movements through the circle. Just calm and gentle movements of the body at peace with itself. The awareness of this free-floating body moving around is all that is needed. Nothing to strive for, no thought or comment, just this.

Nothing to strive for anymore. Then laughter breaks out and the whole group feels the relief of letting go, experiences freedom. No fear, no sadness, no anger, just free-floating, calm movements. Tears of gratitude stream down cheeks. Everything flows in its natural way. This is not a state of mind; this is the authentic self presenting itself in the here and now, a splendid experience that seems to last forever, unlimited by time or space. Just a simple awareness of free-floating authentic self, a self that is always available in the background and that can never disappear. An awesome and overwhelming experience of presence the mind cannot contain or explain. Experiencing awareness itself has this overwhelming quality. Words fail to describe it and yet it is very clear. One could say this is not a state of mind but a state of no-mind. The mind no longer interferes with an experience, and the experience is just experienced as an experience to be experienced.

Desperation and self-compassion

Sarah stepped into the circle. She suffered from psychotic episodes. In these episodes she sometimes found herself screaming in public and could then be picked up by the police and locked up. Sarah, a young woman in her late twenties, was desperate. She felt so disappointed in her life, not being able to have a normal job and a steady relationship with a normal boyfriend. Psychiatric treatments consisted of hospitalization and prescription of psychopharmaceuticals. But the psychotic episodes always returned. When Sarah told her story, her despair resonated with the other participants and they were touched by her story. A true atmosphere of compassion instantaneously appeared. The group could feel in a way what Sarah was experiencing, with her despair and even others things that Sarah was still unaware of.

Sarah was aware of her frustration and anger, and she was very eager to explore them. She hoped that new insights could help her regain her life. The natural reaction of compassion and comfort in the group offered the insight she was looking for. From our experience in the circle, we know that most of the time the moment itself offers a solution to the issue that is raised. Shame, frustration, and self-condemnation are intense feelings that cause a lot of suffering. The natural reaction to suffering is compassion. It was this reaction that Sarah needed to become aware of and allow to happen.

I accompanied Sarah while she was walking through the circle, offering a compassionate reaction by touching her shoulder and staying close to her. Sarah appreciated this gesture and enjoyed my company in the circle. Then I asked Sarah if she knew how to comfort herself. Sarah answered that she did not know how to do that. I suggested that Sarah put her own arms around her shoulders and lay her head on her arm. Sarah agreed, and then she started to cry. Her anger and frustration dissolved and acceptance of her situation as it was arose. She could finally surrender to her sorrow and experience the relief that came from her accepting her vulnerability just as it is. Sarah told us that she hadn't experienced these feelings of vulnerability for a long time. It reminded her of her childhood and the caring touch of her mother. Self-acceptance and self-compassion have this healing quality. There is no need for further exploration or explanation. Just allowing acceptance and compassion to happen is sufficient. The vulnerability remains and needs to be integrated as a helpful quality instead of a threatening experience.

A fearful mind and loving awareness

Love yourself and be awake, today, tomorrow, always.
(Jack Kornfield)

A fearful mind will narrow the space of the individual. Fear is the basic emotion of the mind; fear perpetuates the mind. Mind and fear cooperate and are necessary conditions for each other's existence. The mind tries to prevent a fearful event from happening. But by focusing on the possibility of the fearful situation, the mind emphasizes fear. A second goal of the mind is pleasure. The mind treats pleasure in much the same way as it treats fear; the mind creates a set of rules for pleasure to appear again, a set of rules we know as pleasurable habits, habits we are attached to and we want to have fulfilled over and over again. In an extreme form, habits can become addictions. If we look at this process of executing a habit, we can see that as soon as a habit is affected, the mind will instantaneously create feelings of fear with matching stories that something pleasurable is about to be lost. We like the habits the mind so gently created for us, and no one should be allowed to interfere with them. If someone does interfere, we act as if we accept this interference for the moment, but then we restore the habit as soon as we are in our own habitat. The mind is a true generator of safety and pleasure-seeking behavior. The mind does a great job at this. This behavior is completely automated. The habit just happens as a conditioned reaction to internal or external stimuli. We don't need to be aware of the habit happening.

The basic force of consciousness is love. A consciousness filled with love gives self-confidence and self-appreciation. A loving mind is without fear and acts conducively, creating space for the individual. Noticing and recognizing basic feelings is of tremendous help for the individual to develop a calm state of mind.

When a disturbance of our state of mind appears and it is recognized as fear, we are invited to welcome fear as it is, accepting and allowing it to exist in the moment, to appear and disappear, without acting upon it. We observe fear and see what is causing fear to appear. From this state of spacious awareness we know what actions are to be taken and we can fulfill them. When love appears and is recognized as love, we allow love to fulfill our lives and enjoy its existence in our lives. When fear is recognized and accepted from a perspective of spacious awareness, it will dissolve. When love is recognized it will grow.

Addiction, a dangerous collaboration of body and mind

Come, come, wherever you are, even though you've broken your vows a thousand times, come, come again. (Rumi)

Dora is a woman in her mid-fifties who attended our practice for mental health. For decades she had suffered from ADHD and a severe addiction to alcohol. She used alcohol as a form of self-medication. In the course of time, she consulted several mental health practitioners. She had been abstaining from alcohol for almost fifteen years, but by the time she consulted our practice, she had had several relapses and her family and friends insisted that she should seek serious help. And she too was convinced that she should seek help.

Dora had a good reputation as an actress, and many people enjoyed her eloquent performances. When performing, she had a good focus and there was no longing for alcohol. She was fully in focus. But in daily life with its numerous distractions, she felt this constant restlessness. For as long as she could remember, she had struggled to calm her mind and longed for a moment of rest in her head. With great discipline, she attended meditation workshops and learned to sit still for hours. But still the restlessness remained and never vanished for good. It was the same with her discipline for learning a script for the stage. She could be busy for hours repeating the text until she discovered the right tone, the right rhythm, and the right diction, but sadly enough this state of mind did not last long. As soon as she stopped studying, she lost her focus and the restlessness reappeared. It seemed that despite her efforts and her struggle she was doomed to lose.

From her experience, she knew that alcohol was a real game changer. She learned that only a few sips of her favorite liquor (vodka) sufficed to create this boundless state of mind in which she was no longer hindered by her restless thoughts. Even though she was aware of the long-term negative effects of alcohol – loss of focus and control, withdrawal symptoms, and health problems – she had no good alternative to calm her restless mind.

The treatment Dora received was focused on applying mindfulness and awareness in daily life. Almost every aspect of her daily life was attended to; the relationship with her family, friends, and lovers, her work as an actress, her house, how she behaved in public transport, the collaboration with her colleagues. After several months of weekly sessions, Dora became more and more enthusiastic. For instance, she discovered that the connection with her close relatives was always there and that she did not have to do anything special to experience that connection. She discovered that by validating the connection with her loved ones, a certain calm appeared in that relationship. There seemed nothing more to strive for, just accepting the fact that the connection is there despite the differences in opinion and attitude. She learned how to validate her body and focus her awareness on her body and how her mind became calm while focusing on the movement of the breath in the body. She was a true fan of applying awareness in daily life.

But the fear of relapse into alcohol addiction remained there in the background. One could say that this fear is indeed very functional, and that one should welcome the fear as a helpful resource for preventing relapse.

Here we have to leave the case of Dora for a moment and let me try to clarify something about the mechanisms that make addiction so hard to cope with. What is happening when someone becomes addicted? How is it possible that something that starts so nicely with the attractive experience of feeling good can become such a self-destructive path for the individual? What is happening in the mind and what is happening in the body? Obviously, the body experiences a pleasurable and attractive feeling. In the case of alcohol, you become looser, less bothered by worry, more optimistic and relaxed. (An effect that by the way will vanish as you drink more glasses; then your mind becomes dull and your mood melancholic or euphoric.) Your mind will notice these pleasant changes, and whatever kind of behavior is performed at that moment will be positively rewarded and conditioned. Your mind will seek opportunities to continue that behavior, the intake of alcohol. As long as the rewarding consequences are there, the mind will seek continuation. This is a process of operant conditioning. The mind will seek new opportunities and create thoughts that articulate the positive effect of the intake of alcohol; in a way, the mind is doing its best to help the individual get comfortable. In that way, one might say that the mind is just doing what it is supposed to do, comfort the individual. The mind is happy to fulfill its task and creates an illusion of control; everything is going right, needs are fulfilled, and the individual is happy at that moment. The mind is not busy with the long-term effects of the intake of alcohol. That is obviously one of the effects; after a few glasses, the mind is no longer thinking clearly. Alongside the rewarding aspects of this operant conditioning process in the mind that results in an illusion of control, another even stronger process of classical conditioning is happening in the body.

The body has to learn to get used to the intake of alcohol. It takes learning time to become an experienced drinker. For the sake of the argument and clarification, let's take a look at the experienced drinker. The experienced body gets the signal from the mind that an intake of alcohol will follow. The body anticipates the intake of the toxic substance and, willing or not, has to try to minimize the negative effects of the intake. The body does this by creating a compensatory state in the body. This so-called anticipatory compensatory response is the result of classical conditioning. What this means is that as soon as the body gets the signal from the mind or from the environment that alcohol intake is imminent, the body will react. Just as Pavlov's dog reacted with a salivary reflex to the sound of the bell, so will the experienced drinker react as soon as he or she is in the usual drinking environment or as the drinker anticipates being there. As soon as the plan is made, the body will react with a craving response. The individual can postpone the intake but inevitably the intake will come, sooner or later. And during the intake the body goes on trying to compensate, a compensation that is only handled with more and more intake of alcohol. That's why I call this a dangerous collaboration. Body and mind seem to strive for only one thing: more alcohol. A dramatic course of events and a seemingly unstoppable process, a slippery slope one could best try to avoid by not becoming an experienced drinker.

What are we missing here? Is it really all about body and mind? Has awareness left the stage and left the drinker to surrender to a dark play of mind and body while drinking awareness goes to the background? And though the drinker can be more or less aware of the drinking, awareness is too cloudy and one can no longer observe in a clear way and inspire the mind to make the right decisions. While drinking, there is no role for awareness. Conditioned mind and conditioned body take over. The conditioned reactions of body and mind are simply too strong.

Let's go back to the case of Dora. In the session, we explored how her body was re-acting to the thought of a relapse. Dora noticed the appearance of anxiety, an anxiety that vanished once she realized her firm decision to stay sober and she re-membered her experience with a long period of abstinence that gave her self-confi-dence. Those thoughts reassured her, and her anxiety vanished. Then we explored craving. Could she remember, in the period when she was drinking, how through the day she planned the intake of alcohol and how this thought gave her a good feeling in the body? Just the plan was enough to create this nice feeling. Dora re-membered that vividly, and she told me how it was easy for her to postpone the in-take as long as she knew that the intake would follow. I asked her to go back to such a situation and imagine a plan for intake. As soon as she did this, a nice feeling oc-curred in her body. But when she realized that the intake was not going to come, a very uncomfortable feeling appeared, a feeling that she preferred to escape from and from which escape was not possible. The feeling just appeared. From her expe-rience, she knew that the quick solution would be found in having a glass of alco-hol, and it seemed that even in the session room, the longing for that response was activated. When activating this response, the fear of relapse was activated too. I asked Dora to expose herself in her imagination to the provoking situation of alco-hol intake without performing the conditioned intake of alcohol. Her body could only react with a craving for alcohol. I asked Dora to observe the reactions in her body just as they were, just to bring her awareness to the reactions in her body and keep it there. While exposing herself to the uncomfortable craving reactions in her body, she noticed a decrease. The craving reactions became less uncomfortable and in the end disappeared. Her body could not react otherwise in the confrontation with the eliciting thought of an intake of alcohol. It was her awareness of the sen-sations in her body and the acceptance of these sensations just as they were that made the difference.

However firm the decision for abstinence, the thoughts about re-lapse will reoccur. You simply can't control these thoughts. What you *can* do is bring your awareness to the reactions in the body, accept and investigate these reactions without becoming involved in or overwhelmed by them. Imagine yourself in your favorite drinking spot having a drink. Your body will react as if the intake is about to come. Keep imagining yourself in that spot; your body will anticipate the intake of alcohol and try to minimize the effect of the intake. You will notice a slight uncomfortable feeling while not having the intake. You will notice a slight craving response. While exposing yourself to these craving responses, your body will learn something new, that these craving responses come and go and there is no need for another intake. Your body can bear this craving. Even though your mind is telling you how nice and pleasurable the intake of alcohol would be, you can just decide to bear the uncomfortable feeling. And notice that your body in the end returns to a neutral state. If you want to change your drinking habits, this is a simple and challenging exercise. As long as you distance yourself from the reactions and keep observing, the chance of identification with these craving reactions is minimized. Here you need awareness to create a beneficial change. Body and mind are subject to strong conditioning processes; the unconditioned awareness is needed to make the change.

Loneliness

If one could possess, grasp and know the other,
it would not be other. (Emmanuel Levinas)

One of the saddest stories the mind can tell us is the story of loneliness. In that story the separate self becomes aware of its own
state of isolation and labels it as loneliness. We need connection
with others. We are born out of connection, and without the care
of significant others we cannot survive. Connection with a significant and caring other is a deeply felt need in our lives. As babies,
we reach out to the mother seeking her attention. In a healthy relationship the mother responds with love to the baby's attention
seeking. As babies, we need the caring attention of the mother.
Unsafe attachments in childhood are a very probable cause of a
state of loneliness as an adult. The so-called 'still face' experiment
shows clearly that if the mother stops responding, the baby will
try everything it has in its power to get her attention. If the baby
fails because the mother reacts with a still face without any facial
expression, the baby panics. As babies, we need the caring attention of the mother. Unsafe attachments in childhood are a very
probable cause of a state of loneliness in grown-ups.

How does this state of loneliness develop? The mind notices that attention-seeking behavior elicits unfriendly responses and minimizes communication with significant others. The mind creates a virtual space where others cannot reach the individual. Doors and windows are closed; communication is minimized. In this state of isolation a confident self-image can be preserved. Later in life this solution becomes a problem. By closing down affectionate communication, withdrawing into its own safe space, the separate self excludes intimacy. The mind creates stories about others, blaming them for ignoring the individual, blaming them for ignoring me. It assumes a cynical attitude toward its social environment, and by doing so, it creates even more distance. People can start to avoid that person, and the lonely person becomes lonelier. Loneliness creates a lot of suffering. The sad thing is that only this person can break through this vicious circle. In the state of loneliness we are isolated and live our lives in a seemingly hostile world. Self-hate maintains this state. No one is allowed to come close and see the vulnerability of this isolated self.

The necessary conditions for intimacy are vulnerability and self-disclosure. In an intimate state the experience of a separate self dissolves. In a way, the intimate experience conflicts with what the mind is striving for: control. In the intimate state the mind is not in control but surrenders itself to the intimate experience with the other. The intimate experience with the other has a healing quality for the self. In intimacy we experience the intimate other as an intimate experience; the other is no longer a person with features, an object, but becomes a subjective experience. The other appears in our own intimate circle of awareness. We are aware of the intimate other just as we are aware of our own breath. In our own intimate circle of awareness there are no thoughts, no stories to be told, just experiences to be experienced. In that intimate moment the other is no longer a person we have opinions about. We experience love with the intimate other. This is an experience that comes with thoughts and feelings but is not caused by thoughts and feelings. Thoughts and feelings cannot contain the experience of love. There is no reason for love to exist. There is no 'why' to answer for love. Thought cannot explain love, and feelings are too simple for love. Love is just there, and we know love from our experience just as we know consciousness from our experience.

Intimacy starts in our own selves with self-acceptance. This means allowing yourself to be just as you are. No longer rejecting yourself but just pure acceptance.

> Victor, a man in his late thirties, stepped into the circle. He came to an open mindfulness group one evening with the issue he wanted to explore which was his loneliness. Victor moved awkwardly through the circle, telling about his lonely life and how he longed for a spouse. This was an inspiring issue and in that moment, I had an odd impulse that I decided to follow. I asked Victor whether he had a lure to call his lover to him. Victor looked amazed and shook his head that he didn't have a lure. I explained that birds use a lure to find their spouses. They sit in a tree and sing their lure. So maybe this is how Victor could find his spouse too. He could just sing her to him. The other participants reacted with the same amazement. I asked Victor again whether he could try to find his lure while walking through the circle. Victor agreed and started walking, uttering a few sounds, and then he stopped, explaining that this wasn't working for him. He wasn't succeeding, and it was painful for him and the others to observe how he was trying and failing at this task. Then I asked Victor whether he ever dreamed of her. Victor nodded that he did. So I asked him to walk through the circle and tell her that he dreamed of her. Victor

started walking and said, 'I dream of you, I long for you, I dream of you, I dream of you, please let me find you.' His voice grew louder and his step became stronger. The circle was filled with admiration for this strong Victor who emerged out of this search for his lure. A self-confident man now walked in the circle. Right in his own heart he found the lure for his future lover, and he was about to follow his heart. This was the only time Victor visited the circle and it seemed to be enough. It happens often that people visit the circle once and later, on other occasions, I hear from them how a beneficial change has occurred.

Noticing, naming, and containing

The world is all there is. (Ludwig Wittgenstein)

In the circle we ask participants if they are aware of the feelings that appear, and if so, if they can allow their feelings to take the floor and show the feelings as they are. We notice the feelings and accept their appearance. When there is a tendency to hide the feelings, we gently invite them to show themselves. We observe how participants try to ignore their feelings, and we invite them to live the feelings and recognize them and play with them. Noticing, naming, and containing are important ingredients of the circle of awareness. Noticing, naming, and containing help us to see the true nature of the feelings. We notice a disturbance of the mood, recognize it as an emotion, and accept its existence, but we don't act upon it. That's not necessary. We don't analyze it either. Whenever the feelings are there, the story is no longer necessary. The story is allowed to disappear and leave the stage to the feelings. By shifting our attention from story to feelings, thoughts will evaporate and disappear. Thought will act reluctantly — we understand that — as thought likes to take the floor and explain why feelings are there, but actually feelings are already there and don't need an explanation. Explanation of feeling is just an implicit justification for thought's own existence. This is an understandable attempt of thought to take over, and this is something that will happen over and over. So we gently focus on our feelings and ask these feelings to show themselves so we can observe their true nature. We see that feelings stream. When we allow them to flow freely, we see that feelings are an expression of energy, a forecast of change that is about to happen.

When an issue is raised, thought will tell the story of being stuck in circumstances and conditions. Thought repeats that story over and over and is convinced that there are no possibilities for desirable change. The only change that will happen, so thought tells us, is a worsening of the circumstances. So thought will continue to blame the circumstances and hinder any possibility for change to occur.

> A young woman named Vicky stepped into the circle and told the story of her unemployment. She was desperate and cynical. Her hope for positive change was gone. During the week, she stayed at home avoiding social contacts and blaming herself for not having a proper job. Vicky was in an agitated mood as she told us how disappointed and frustrated she was. I asked her whether she was aware of her agitation and invited her to become even more aware of her agitation by intensifying her feelings of agitation. Vicky agreed and started to express her agitation. In the middle, she wanted to explain the reason for her agitation by telling a story about the bureaucracy and all the paperwork she had to go through. I asked her instead to intensify her agitated movements of arms and legs, allowing her to express all the emotions with her body. Just to allow feelings to stream through her body without acting upon them. After a few rounds through the circle, a quiet and almost serene calmness came over her. Something had changed. The circumstances of her unemployment remained the same, but Vicky had changed. Her self-con-

demning thoughts went to the background. She became aware of a new insight in-
to who she was and where opportunities for her were available. With this new
insight she felt more self-confident and capable of coping with her situation.

Noticing, naming, and containing are the key ingredients for allowing change to happen. Emotions and feelings need to be recognized as such. Then, after acknowledging and containing the emotions, the energy that the emotions are made of becomes available to the individual. Containment of emotions is necessary. Contain them, instead of explain them. By containing them we have the conscious choice about how to cope with the situation. We can be easily overwhelmed by the force of emotions and dramatize our situation. Drama is the result of the unconscious collaboration of emotion and thought, and in drama we are convinced of the truth of our interpretation of what is happening. This truth becomes even truer because of the intensity of the emotion. But emotion is just vital energy taking the form of an emotion, an energy form floating through our body-mind system, and we can use this energy for our own advantage if we are overwhelmed by it. 'You can't stop the waves, but you can learn how to surf them' is a famous metaphor explaining how this works. With this metaphor in mind we can easily understand how to cope with emotions. They are just energy. As we cannot separate the wave from the ocean, we cannot separate emotion from vital energy. A feeling is a conscious emotion; if we add awareness to an emotion, the emotion becomes a feeling. By noticing an emotion and acknowledging it by labeling it as a feeling like anger, fear, or joy and then allowing its existence without putting it into further action, emotion can stream back to the ocean of vital energy. The temporary form of emotion will dissolve back into this pure energy, and from this energy a new emotion can arise. If we can see emotions as reactions from our body-mind system — to stimuli from the outer perceptual world or the inner world of thoughts — and realize that emotions will not and cannot last forever, we can observe emotions as they are and see them come and go.

Let's take an everyday example. Suppose you are in a rush and have to go to the grocery store to do some quick shopping. You collect your products for the day and go to the cashier. You look for the shortest line, and after making your choice you find yourself in the wrong one. The cashier is slow and the client in front of you in the queue starts a discussion with the cashier about the price of a product. The cashier calls for the manager etc. In that situation many of us will experience annoyance. Annoyance is something that can overwhelm you and provoke a cascade of thoughts, emotions, and gestures. Annoyance of course is just an emotional reaction. By recognizing it as a reaction and labeling it as annoyance, we can learn to contain this emotional reaction as it is, without further judgment and without further reaction. We can act non-reactively and may find ourselves able to smile at the situation. Daily life is good practice for observing these kinds of processes. Daily life with its numerous temptations helps us to become aware and to de-automate ourselves. Noticing, naming, and containing helps. For the conditioned mind daily life is a constant justification of the conditioned convictions the mind has about the world and itself. Riding through the traffic in the city, visiting a supermarket, collaborating with colleagues — daily life is full of possibilities for the justification of our core beliefs. Core beliefs and emotions are entangled and form a cause for each other. By disentangling core beliefs and emotions, they can go back to the ocean they came from.

When an issue arises in our awareness and attracts our attention, it provokes our action. It will then seem that something needs to be done. Mind is always trying to control the vital energy with conditioning. The method we describe here invites us not to go into a reaction but to stay with our attention only. The act of disentangling thought and emotion is a powerful tool to free the underlying energy and allow our vital force to stream.

Losing control

John, a man in his mid-forties, stepped into the circle and wanted to explore his tendency to control his life in all kinds of ways. He was dissatisfied with it and trying to improve his situation by analyzing it over and over again and trying to find new solutions. He had worked hard and finally concluded that none of his solutions would work. He was unemployed and sought new perspectives in his life. In the circle he presented his tendency toward rational control and his body moved in a rigid way while he quickly and intelligently responded to the questions of the trainer. Intellectually there was nothing wrong with him, and he was eager to demonstrate this with quick and smart answers, tempting me to join him in an intellectual debate. I responded by asking John to observe how his body was moving and whether he could experience the stiffness of his body. I asked him whether or not his body felt comfortable to him. Several suggestions were given to John about how to facilitate the awareness of his body. John responded rationally, explaining how he thought his body felt. As an experienced meditator his responses seemed adequate. We saw however that his body kept moving in a restrained way. Whenever the mind takes control, the body can reflect this restrained, less elegant and less spontaneous way of moving around. It seemed like John was cooperating with the process of exploration, but actually his mind was challenging the trainer to join him in a philosophical and spiritual debate over the issue he raised about how he could follow his own path.

His mind seemed to be in full control, yet his body moved inflexibly. This is not the nature of the body, the body by its nature wants to move freely. If we watch carefully, there is almost always some unattended part of the body moving freely; a leg is rocking, fingers are drumming, or a face is smiling. If we look carefully, the body shows where freedom is being experienced. In John's case, it was his right thumb. John was facing me, as the trainer. He seemed willing to cooperate with the process of exploration while at the same time challenging me to join him in a debate. His hands were behind his back. I wasn't able to see whether or not his hands were moving. When I asked John what was happening behind his back, he replied that there were only his hands. Then I asked the other participants what was happening behind John's back, and they said that while John was talking, his right thumb was moving up and down. I suggested to John that he join me in an experiment. We would go on debating the spiritual issues John raised, and meanwhile the other participants would observe the movements of his thumb, as it seemed John wasn't aware of his moving thumb. Those movements were beyond mind control. It was like his thumb was responding in a different way than his thoughts, different from what he said. The participants went on to observe the movements of John's thumb and John went on with his debate. While John was talking and stating that he felt calm, his thumb was moving nervously in the opposite way. When John received this feedback and noticed how the movement of his thumb was beyond his control, a shift in his apparently calm state occurred. His body started to shake as though energy was coming loose. This lasted for some time, and I asked John to stay with it and focus his attention on his body. Then, after some time, a true calmness came over John. Finally his mind had given up control, allowing energy to float freely through his body. John felt very relieved afterwards. He was amazed about the tremendous amount of energy that was floating through his body and was available just for him. For that moment he had experienced freedom from his mind control and had enjoyed the experience. John became a loyal participant of the circle and experienced on more occasions inside and outside the circle a calm state of mind just by letting go of his control.

What we see in the case of John is the appearance of the natural flow of energy through the body. This energy is known by several names: kundalini, prana, orgone, and cosmic energy. Most of the time, this energy is accompanied by spontaneous shaking and trembling of the whole body. The rise and fall of this energy is a natural and spontaneous process that can be facilitated but not evoked by will. The energy is rising and the mind is no longer resisting. New forms can arise out of this energy.

Thoughts are very intimate to the self, they seem to reveal who we really are. We can say friendly words to a person and at the same time disapprove of this person with our thoughts. This is just a trivial example. We do this all the time, not because we enjoy doing it, but because we are accustomed to doing so. We are accustomed to hiding our inner thoughts and keeping them to ourselves. Thoughts have an ultimate intimate quality, and based on this experience we identify ourselves with our thoughts. Thoughts seem to reveal who we really are. Our true self seems to be hidden in our thoughts. If there is one place we should feel safe, it should be in the intimacy of our thoughts. We find no one else in our thoughts other than our own selves. Thoughts come and go. We don't know where they go and we don't know where they come from. In this way, thoughts are just like other appearances, they just appear, like sounds, tastes, smells, etc. Thoughts appear and we perceive them like other appearances, and like these other appearances we don't necessarily cause them ourselves. As we are not in control of our bodily sensations or feelings, we are not in control of our thoughts. Thoughts don't listen to our instructions; if for instance we don't want to think about something, thoughts about that something pop up all the time.

Most of the time we think rather neutrally, and we hardly notice what we are thinking. Sometimes we think thoughts that we don't want to think but still we do. Thoughts are then beyond our control, and these thoughts can have a dark enigmatic quality just like our dreams can have. Thoughts are easily confused with awareness itself. Sometimes it seems that all awareness truly is about what we are thinking. Our awareness has narrowed itself around thinking. It can seem like thoughts can claim our attention as a superior process that can comment on the world in and around us and reveal our true self, but if we look more closely, we can see that this is not true. Thought exaggerates its own importance. Just like bodily sensations and feelings, thoughts just happen. We experience our thinking as we experience our tasting. We taste a flavor and we think a thought. Both are experiences. We don't need to analyze these phenomena; we can choose just to experience them. Then we can learn to know our thoughts as we know the leaves on a tree, the clouds in the sky; just as phenomena happening. We don't need to taste the flavor again to be aware of it, we can just taste the taste. We don't need to think a thought again, we can just think the thought. We can just observe the occurrence of a thought and see how our body reacts, just as we can observe a taste and see how our body reacts. The 'letting go' of thoughts can be very hard to practice for some people.

You are not your thoughts

The case of Simon tells us another story of mind control. This is the story of overidentification with thought processes and the development of shame. Simon was afraid of his own thoughts. Simon was a young bookkeeper who was suffering from intrusive thoughts about harming his loved ones. He was very ashamed of the content of his thoughts and could not live with them anymore. He hated his thoughts, and because his thoughts shared him all the time that he was his thoughts, he hated himself. Simon sought individual counseling because he was so ashamed he did not dare to express his thoughts in the open space of a circle. He was convinced that his thoughts were so bad and that he was unique in having these terrible thoughts. The first time he shared these thoughts in an individual session, he felt deeply ashamed and was afraid of becoming mad. The contents of his thoughts were images of him killing his fiancée with a knife. He was shocked and terrified by this thought and wondered how he was even capable of thinking this. He was convinced that these thoughts were actually proof of his total worthlessness, and this conclusion frightened him even more. I asked Simon what he felt in his body while talking about his thoughts. Simon was surprised by this question and started to explain how frightened he was and what kind of bad person he must be. He believed he should be rejected and isolated from his loved ones because he was a real danger to them. I repeated the question, inviting Simon to observe his body. Simon did so and revealed that he felt deep disgust and stress all over his body. His body was reacting strongly and in a very clear way. His body tried to get rid of these terrible thoughts and at the same time Simon began to give attention to those thoughts. Simon needed to become aware of the reaction of his body and listen to it.

The reaction of his body clearly showed that these thoughts did not fit with him. As long as Simon gave attention to the thoughts and tried to analyze why he was thinking this way, Simon would re-expose his body to these very unattractive stimuli and in reaction, the body would try to get rid of them. Thoughts just happen and the body can't escape from thoughts, but the body does react to them and in this case with disgust, just like a body reacts to food that it does not like. Disgust is a quite clear reaction that says a lot about the thing the body is reacting to. If a thing or stimulus does not fit with the body, the body simply wants to escape from it. Just by observing the body we know a lot. So what does the reaction of the body to these thoughts tell us about these thoughts? The answer is of course that these thoughts do not fit with the body and so these thoughts did not fit with Simon. These thoughts were truly not any good for the body and were truly not good for Simon. This explanation and demonstration was a breakthrough for Simon. Now he knew that these thoughts, no matter how intimate they were, did not belong to him. Thinking thoughts is not the same as performing an action. Thoughts are not to be confused with actions, they are totally different. Actually, it is quite normal for people to have all kinds of intrusive thoughts about harming others or performing sexual actions with others and it becomes a problem if we start to fight those thoughts because then they become stronger. The anxiety in these thoughts comes from the misconception that we are what we think. Like we are not the smell in our nose, or the sounds in our ear, we are not the thoughts in our thinking. What we perceive is not who we are.

After this session Simon felt a great relief and started to practice observing his bodily reactions. About a year later I received an e-mail from Simon that things were going well. The intrusive thoughts had disappeared for the most part. He and his his fiancée had bought a beautiful house and now he was having all kinds of worries that were troubling him. Simon was questioning himself, wondering whether he had made a good decision and if he and his fiancée really were a good match. He was afraid of a relapse and sought advice.

'As promised I was to write a postcard about how I was doing. Just an update. The last months have gone very well. I only had a few nasty thoughts, and when they appeared I knew how to handle them. But recently we bought a beautiful house in the city and now I find myself again thinking these nasty thoughts and doubting our relationship. Is my fiancée the right woman for me?' Simon received the following answer: 'It's so good to hear that you did well in handling your thoughts. Your practice has improved. In a stressful situation like you are in right now, your mind is working hard to keep control by activating old patterns again. This is what the mind does. In this case your thoughts are pointing to your dysfunctional belief suggesting that you are not acting in a proper way and you are not good enough. Your thoughts are never able to prove your love for your fiancée. Love is something you experience and not something you think. You feel love, that's it. The simple fact that you feel terrible because of your doubtful thoughts proves, as we discussed earlier, that these thoughts don't fit with you.' Simon replied: 'Thanks a lot for your e-mail. How funny that just a few words can give so much energy and calm. I'll go on. Thanks again.'

The story goes on. Two years later, during a period of huge changes in his personal life, Simon had a relapse in his obsessive intrusions and was referred to me again.

Simon was in a panic and feared that his horrifying thoughts would never disappear again and that he was doomed to live with them. His social and professional life had changed. He had a new partner, and he was very enthusiastic about his new love. And he had made a firm career step in his professional life. Everything seemed to be going well and maybe his mind was afraid of losing control and started to create all kinds of intrusive thoughts to keep Simon in an over-alert state. In the sessions to follow, we repeated the successful exposure to the content of his thoughts and discussed that they were just thoughts. The mere fact that Simon was reacting with repulsion was indeed a good sign that these thoughts did not fit him. We explored that Simon was not his thoughts and that he should not confuse his actual actions with his thoughts. As an alternative treatment for his panic, we discussed the possibility of an anxiolytic in case Simon could not cope with his fear. That evening his girlfriend asked Simon how things had gone during his visit with his psychotherapist. Simon told her that he felt relief after the session, and in an attempt to explain to her where this relief came from, he told her about how thoughts can mislead. He explained to her that for instance he could think that he was a cowboy, but that thinking the thought of him being a cowboy would not make him a cowboy. He told her to just look at him and notice that he didn't change into a cowboy. In that very moment – when Simon heard himself explaining to his girlfriend that he was not a cowboy – he realized that he was indeed not his thoughts. It was like the sky opened and everything became clear.

At our next session Simon was very enthusiastic. It was as if he could finally look behind his thoughts and notice they are just thoughts.

Training awareness

Breathing in, I calm body and mind. Breathing out, I smile.
Dwelling in the present moment, I know this is the only
moment. (Thich Nhat Hanh)

Let's go back to breathing and explore what is happening there.
As we can experience, breathing is just happening. We can learn
to observe the movement of the breath in our body and notice
that it is not us who is doing the breathing. We experience the
movement and can notice that with or without our thinking, the
breathing is just happening. The movement in the body comes
and goes without the interference of the thinking mind. With or
without the comment of the mind, breathing is there. One might
wonder who is doing the breathing? And if we look for this
someone, there is no one to be found. Of course we are very
aware of the importance of breathing for our life. It is in a true
sense our reason for being. So who is in charge of our breathing?
There is no one to find. Even though breathing is of utmost importance, no one is really doing it. Breathing just happens to be
there. Most of the time we don't even notice it. We only become
aware of breathing when we are stuffed up. Stuffy moments are
far from neutral and require a proper action to restore healthy
breathing. In other moments we are hardly aware of breathing at

all. The mindfulness approach invites us to explore our neutral breathing not with the aim to change it, but with the aim to gain insight into our true nature and discover that breathing is not something that is done by ourself but is just there as part of our natural being. Breathing most of the time is not a volitional act or process. It is just happening by itself for itself, as an intrinsic part of life. This mindful breathing as we can call it is an important introductory tool to the circle. Developing a neutral stance to processes that emerge in our awareness is crucial for the further exploration of what is truly happening. In any situation where we get overwhelmed by an experience, we can return to this neutral experience of breathing in and breathing out, even if it is only for a moment, and create distance from the experience that is overwhelming us. Not as another exercise for improving our breathing process but for reminding ourselves of the possibility of this neutral stance. Whatever emerges in our awareness cannot be changed in that moment. It cannot be improved. It is already there, and it can only be accepted as just another experience. We start with the breathing process because breathing is the very core of our existence. Even though breathing is of utmost importance, as a daily experience it is happening in the background of our awareness. Through the day we are hardly aware of the breathing process. It is a neutral process and does not need our attention to be fulfilled. We take this neutral process to become more aware of the possibility for our own neutrality and quiet state of mind. A possibility that is always there and available to us. So we shift our attention from daily hassles to the process of breathing. If the process of breathing is compromised by fear, we just shift the attention to another neutral process of the body, like the sensations of our feet touching the floor. Again we do this not as an exercise to improve the noticing of the texture of your feet touching the ground but as an exercise to experience the neutral-ity of this observation. Mindful breathing, mindful walking, mindful sitting is all about being aware and developing a neutral state of mind, then applying this state of mind in other situations. By applying this neutral state of mind in more challenging situa-tions, we can see more clearly the opportunities these situations offer.

Thought will tell us that we have to be alert to cope with these challenging situations. It will tell us that we have to be alert all the time to prevent something bad from happening. Awareness will tell us just to be aware, be fully present here and now and notice the opportunities hidden in this moment waiting to be seen.

In the circle we start with learning to observe in a neutral way, to observe from moment to moment without judgment. Once we are able to observe the breathing process in a neutral way, we can see when a distraction appears. We notice the distraction and la-bel it as distraction, then we gently bring our attention back to the movement of the breathing in the body. By practicing this, we develop a neutral stance and a neutral state of mind in which it is easier to see the nature of distraction. We can see how something is coming to our awareness, and we notice the appearance of this new experience. In that very moment, there is the possibility of making a conscious choice to give our attention to this new expe-rience. This is easy for daily sensations like the sound of a car passing by or voices of people in the other room. The experience of hearing these new sounds and the decision to pay no further attention to them is easy to fulfill. Those experiences are almost neutral and they don't trigger an emotional reaction. The next step in the training process from the circle is to apply the neutral observational stance to emotional reactions that appear and observe how emotions create reactions in our bodies. Participants are asked to activate a memory of a situation where they felt uncomfortable and reacted with dysfunctional emotional behavior. Any situation will do as long as participants found for themselves that they reacted dysfunctionally. Emotions put us and our environment in action. Emotions by their nature evoke motion. The primary function of emotions is to evoke motion and create change as an effect. Functional emotions create useful changes in our environment or in ourselves. Emotions have an important communicative aspect. People will understand each other's intentions better if an emotion is being expressed.

Observing a change in mood

John was a man in his late forties. For decades, he had been suffering from severe depressive moods. He was working successfully as a scientist in a research lab, was married to a loving wife, and had beautiful children. On the surface, he was functioning well and had every reason to be happy. But still his depressive moods were always there in the background and returned regularly to disturb his life. John sought several treatments through the years. He was treated with antidepression medication combined with cognitive behavioral therapy. And though John took his medication faithfully and followed the advice of his therapist carefully, John did not recover and relapsed regularly into his depressive moods. His psychiatrist finally referred him to the Mental Health Group (GGZgroep) in Amsterdam for a treatment with rTMS. This is a well-documented experimental treatment where electromagnetic impulses are applied to the head of the patient in order to reset cortical networks in the brain. In a way, the cortical networks are reset to a more neutral state and are more open to process new, more functional cognitive ideas. This is the reason why rTMS is offered in parallel to supportive psychotherapeutic sessions with the patient. John benefitted from this approach, and his scores on a scale that measures depression improved.

Then, during one session, John reported that even though his mood was much better in general during the week, he still suffered from severe depressive moods on the weekend. He could almost set his clock by the reappearance of his depressive mood. Saturday afternoon he and his family were gathered together having a cozy time and out of the blue, the depressive mood announced its arrival. There was nothing

John could do to prevent it, and finally he withdrew to his bedroom, waiting for several hours for his mood to return to bearable again. When he couldn't fit in with his family anymore and to spare them and him the pain of this experience, the only solution John could find was to withdraw to his bedroom. While John was telling his touching story, I knew of course that it would be of utmost importance to validate his depressive mood and disappointment. Carefully we sought the right words to express his experience. And we found descriptions like 'John was overwhelmed by a dark cloud that hung over him like a big black umbrella' and 'no spark of light entered his awareness.' His whole experience was infused with this omnipresent heavy mood. It was like all joy and satisfaction were drawn out of him. No escape was possible. He was completely surrounded by this sad darkness. We agreed that this was precisely what was happening and John indeed couldn't do anything other than withdraw and wait for better times. The depressive mood at those times was in control, and it was understandable that John feared that his depression would gain more control. His despair and fear of relapse were tangible in the consulting room.

Then I asked John what it was in him that knew that his depressive state was there. What was it in him that recognized the reappearance of his depressive mood? John was surprised by my question. For him, it was obvious that in his thoughts he recognized the depressive symptoms and with his thoughts he recognized the return of his depressive mood. It was in his thoughts that he planned to go to his bedroom and wait for better times. That seemed logical. But still the question remained what in him recognized the symptoms. John stated that he noticed the heaviness of his body, the lack of energy etc. The experience of these symptoms was indisputably true and so he knew that his depressive mood had returned. Even so, he knew that he was thinking and that negative thoughts about his mood change were coming to him, thoughts that, whatever effort he made, the depressive mood would return. The experience of him thinking these thoughts and feeling his feelings was just there. This is how he knew that the depression had returned. Again I asked John where it was that this knowledge of this experience resided at the moment, what in him knew this. In further exploring his experiences, John concluded that he was aware of having these thoughts and feeling these feelings and bodily sensations of heaviness and lack of energy. I asked John if experiencing these experiences was for him the same as being aware of them. John was a little surprised when he concluded that his awareness of this experience was not the same as the experience itself. His awareness and his experience of his depressive mood seemed to coincide with each other but were actually not the same. And then John discovered that it was possible to detach from the experience by noticing his awareness of the experience. In observing his experience, he was no longer absorbed by it. The observing and knowing quality of awareness remains independent; even when the experience seemed to overwhelm everything, the awareness remained. I asked John to experiment with this stance the next time his depressive mood returned and to keep on observing the change in mood. We agreed that John would apply this method over the coming weekend.

The next session, John entered the room with a smile on his face and reported that it really worked. As expected, his depressive mood returned, but now he kept on observing. He was no longer overwhelmed and the mood no longer had this vast impact on him. His fear and disappointment diminished, and more quickly than usual his normal mood came back.

Hindrances to awareness

Keep on observing. (Jotika Hermsen)

Awareness by its nature is clear and transparent. This clear awareness shows you things as they are, composed. To see the true nature of the phenomena one needs clear awareness. Traditionally five obstacles to acquiring clear awareness are described, obstacles that are identified as mental factors that hinder progress in your meditation practice. Knowing these obstacles helps you to clear your awareness.

During a winter retreat of Vipassana meditation, my meditation teacher Jotika Hermsen clarified the hindrances with the following ancient metaphor.

A clear mind is like a forest pond. When the pond is clean and the surface is still, you sometimes see oil slicks from the plants below on the water. Beautiful colors that hold your gaze. Or you see a beautiful reflection of the surroundings of the pond on the surface of the water and you are not able to look at the bottom of the pond. This first obstacle is called desire. Your mind is full of desire, seeking more beauty and happiness, and you can't see the depth of your awareness. The second obstacle is when the water of the pond is boiling. The water is heated and bubbles of gas hinder you from seeing the bottom of the pond. This obstacle is known as ill will. No reflection is possible. The mind is full of annoyance and judgment of others. The third obstacle is dullness. You look at the pond and your eye is caught by thick algae growing across the pond. You can look at the bottom of the pond only if you pull out the algae that fill the pond. A very tiring job and you lack the energy for that. The fourth obstacle is restlessness. The wind is churning up the water of the pond and you can't see the bottom. The fifth obstacle is doubt. Doubt is like water filled with mud. The mind is ruminating and full of doubt. You are not able to see clearly.

In the meditation tradition, the advice is to make no important decisions whatsoever when the mind is troubled with hindrances. Just keep observing and the hindrances will dissolve.

Awareness while performing a boring task

Julia is a young psychotherapist taking an intensive face-to-face mindfulness course. One day she brings an issue to the session. She tells me about how she avoids administrative tasks and finds herself delaying these tasks until delay is no longer possible. She feels guilty and irritated by her performance, and she blames herself for being inadequate and lacking professional discipline. Maybe she is not fit for the job if she cannot find the discipline to perform these simple administrative tasks as other professionals seem to do so easily. Julia was working with patients who had serious personality disorders. She loved her work and was delighted and challenged by her complex caseload. She had a great number of responsibilities in her job and was an empathic psychotherapist with deep caring for her patients. But still she delayed administrative tasks until frustration and guilt became too much and she ultimately did her administration. She hated this behavior and noticed that she had behaved in this way for as long as she could remember; delaying tasks, feeling guilty about it, and finally performing them under great pressure. When colleagues confronted her with the tasks that still needed to be done, she would feel even guiltier and start to perform the task with even more ambivalence. As part of her training we looked together at this process of postponement. After Julia explained the situation at work, I asked her to imagine that this *administrative task was a person seeking her attention, trying to make an appointment for a meeting. I asked Julia to suppose that she didn't want to meet this person. Julia revealed that in that case her tendency would be to avoid contact. She would feel a clear 'no' about meeting that person. If that person kept trying to arrange a meeting, Julia would continue to avoid that person. The dynamics of the situation would not change. The person would persist in trying to seek her attention to arrange a meeting and Julia would keep on avoiding. Julia concluded that even if a meeting were unavoidable, she would continue her tendency to avoid contact and try to escape the meeting as soon as possible. During the meeting her attention would wander. Julia agreed that this pattern was the same pattern she performed with the administrative tasks; she would try to avoid them, delay them, and finally perform them reluctantly.*

We noticed in her example the element of self-destructiveness and frustration as an emotion. The self-destructive thoughts explain and justify the emotions of frustration, so it all fitted together well, and Julia became more convinced that she was not performing properly. It was an old pattern she recognized all too well. The bottom line was that even though she loved her work very much, she was not able to perform in a professional way and then it seemed that her true nature of being a failure was revealed again.

Each time a person sought her attention, Julia knew a way to cope with the situation. She had learned her own methods, and her social skills were well developed. She knew how to handle a request from another person or a colleague without feeling guilty or blaming herself for not answering the demands of others. She knew how she could politely postpone a demand from a colleague, for instance, by stating that she heard the request and would act on it within a proper time frame. But she could not yet relate this experience to her pattern of delaying administrative tasks.

What happens when someone seeks our attention? That person enters our field of awareness, and instantaneously we experience like, dislike, or neutral. Someone enters our field who was not there before, and like, dislike, or neutral is immediately there. It does not matter if we are considering a person or an object that is entering our field of awareness, in the experience of like, dislike, or neutral there are no differences whether this perception concerns an object, a person, or a task. Someone or something that was not there before enters our awareness and that is what matters. In our experience something or someone just popped up. It is not relevant whether the person or the thing is actually there, the popping up in our awareness is what matters. Then instantaneously, liking, neutral, or disliking occurs. Even if the person or the thing is not actually around us, even if we think about this someone or something, like or dislike appears. We know from previous experience how we react to that someone or something, and like or dislike is there again in the same way. The actual experience is the experience of like, dislike, or neutral. In that moment, on the basis of that information, we can make the choice how to react further. In that moment, if we are aware of like, dislike, or neutral, we can interfere with the unconscious process of conditioning and decide consciously how to act upon this new arrival in our awareness. It doesn't really make any difference if a person is approaching you or the thought of an administrative task to be performed pops up — like, dislike, or neutral will appear.

> For Julia it became clear that her immediate reaction was one of dislike every time she thought of her administrative tasks. This was an initial response she wasn't aware of, she was only aware of the next step in the process which was her irritation and frustration. Now that she was becoming aware of her initial response of dislike, this allowed her several options for further conscious reactions. For Julia this meant that she could treat her thoughts the same way as she treated an actual person. As the thought seeks her attention just like the person in the example, the process is the same, so she was free to decide how to act upon this thought entering her awareness. She could, for instance, notice her reaction of dislike of this thought and then, after thanking the thought for seeking her attention, she could decide to wait for the right time to reply to the thought. Then her reaction would be neutral and so would her state of mind. She can notice the appearance of thought and not rush too quickly to an answer. You can take your time to consider and contemplate your thoughts, and the right reaction will appear for you.

Like, dislike, and neutral are indisputable. You cannot argue with the taste of your body-mind system. The automated consequences of like and dislike are approach and avoidance. Before the approach or avoidance response occurs, we can interfere. As conscious beings we are able to notice like and dislike. We can notice our tendency to approach or avoidance and decide not to perform these reactions. By acting this way, the vicious circle of the unconscious conditioning process can be broken. An approach to a liked object is a reward for the body-mind system. This is a pleasant experience. Avoiding a disliked object is rewarding too. It makes an unpleasant experience stop. Like and dislike occur in the chain of conditioned responses and are themselves subject to the conditioning process, a process that takes place in the unconscious and is automatic. We can change this process by adding awareness to it. By noticing like or dislike and deciding not to act upon it, we neutralize like and dislike. In former conditioning processes the like and dislike responses were functional for learning certain behavior patterns. In the actual moment these responses and consequent behaviors could become dysfunctional.

Let's have a closer look at Julia who is postponing a boring administrative task. The task came to her attention. She noticed the appearance of the thought about this task. She recognized the boring character and started to avoid it mentally and delay it actually. She discussed in her mind why she did not appreciate the task and told herself that she would fulfill it later. Then she noticed that she had delayed the task several times already. Her guilty feelings arose, and the disliking character of the task grew into even more dislike. This all took place in a context of conditioned responses. The thought of the administrative task appears in a moment. It is suddenly there. We don't know where thoughts come from, and we don't know where they are going. Thoughts happen to come and go, like other stimuli just come and go. We recognize the stimuli and act upon them the same way we have learned to from previous experiences with these kinds of stimuli. In daily life we are hardly aware of our reactions, and most of the time we live on automatic pilot. Thoughts are like other stimuli, and we react to thoughts as we react to perceptual sensations. What a smell is for the nose, a thought is for the mind. Thoughts appear and like, dislike, or neutral is there and gives information about the thought. The information Julia got was that she didn't like the thought of the administrative task. In exploring her process it became crystal clear that the conscious noticing of like or dislike was crucial in order for further steps to be taken. Just like when a person seeks her attention, she can validate the wish of that person to come into contact with her and tell that person that now is an inconvenient time and later on she will look into that wish for contact. It is like deciding to answer a phone call or reply to an e-mail. That decision is hers to make. She is free to decide whether she wants to spend time with another person. Likewise she is free to decide if she wants to perform a task, yes or no, at that particular moment. Even if the thought comes to her mind, it is up to her how to act upon it. So if the thought comes to her mind and she notices the unattractiveness of the thought, she can indeed conclude that this is not the right time for her to act upon the thought. Maybe later at a more convenient moment she would pay attention to this thought. Now the thought did not fit with her peace of mind. She gently decides to look into thinking about the task later. Now the decision to delay the task is hers and not part of unconscious conditioning. She deliberately chooses to delay the task and steps out of the spiral of negative thoughts, guilty feelings, and passivity. In exploring these steps Julia actually experienced a big relief by realizing that she has gained freedom again. Julia was very enthusiastic about this new insight, and later on she communicated that she experienced more freedom and autonomy in her daily life.

Social awareness

All actual life is encounter. (Martin Buber)

Something is entering your awareness and you are aware that this something, a smell, a sound, a thought is entering. In that tiny moment there is the possibility of interfering with the conditioning process. In that very moment when you are aware of like and dislike, you can act consciously instead of continuing on automatic pilot. In the automatic state you will find yourself confirming your learned stories over and over again. The story of social fear is such a story. It is told over and over and steers our lives frequently. As social beings we are all prone to the fear of being excluded from a group of important others. Belonging to a group is of ultimate value.

Nina was a woman in her mid-fifties. She attended group training for psychotherapists. Nina had traveled all around the world, she was successful in her work, and she had a great family life. She had many reasons to feel self-confident and yet she was afraid of speaking in public. She was convinced that others would see her uncertainty and conclude that she was a fake and a failure because she was not even capable of speaking in public. She felt ashamed and while confessing this to the other group members, she was sure they would condemn her for revealing her inner fear. The other group members listened carefully and of course no one condemned Nina for her confession. Nina wasn't aware of the friendly and compassionate attitude of the other group members because she was stuck in her own frightening story and anticipated rejection by the group. That story was the root of her inability to speak in front of a group. She experienced the fear as tension in her body. Her story referred to experiences of social rejection that had happened in the past. In the present situation, nothing frightening happened, but still there was the experience of tension in her body, a rising heart rate and sweat on her body. These internal cues of her body confirmed her fear and were interpreted as a sign that this situation was truly dangerous. I asked Nina to participate in a simple experiment, in this case counting from 1 to 20 in front of the group. Nina agreed to do so. I told her to just count in her own way. The rest of the group was instructed to observe Nina while she did the counting. Nina started the counting task, and with a trembling voice she counted from 1 to 20. When I asked her to evaluate her performance, she said that it was the same as always, she could not even perform this simple task correctly and now the whole group was seeing her failure. She felt ashamed and feared the pity of the group and ultimately rejection. The other group members agreed with her that they could hear her trembling voice while she was performing the counting task and recognized the fearful state she was in. Nina revealed that she felt horrible. She felt tension throughout her body, her heart rate rose and she began to sweat. This process started as soon as she was asked to perform the counting task; the moment she anticipated how she would perform, her body started to react in the usual way. My invitation for this experiment entered her awareness and was immediately responded to with a qualification of dislike. Her emotional reaction and the activation of social rejection stories were part of an overlearned and deeply embedded conditioned pattern. If she wanted to de-condition this pattern, she needed to go deep into her chain of reactions and interfere in the very beginning of that chain where like or dislike started. I asked Nina to perform the same task again, and while performing the counting task, to focus on the counting itself. Before she started counting, I asked Nina to observe the steps in her process and to begin counting when she could accept these reactions just as they are. While counting, when she began to be distracted by her bodily sensations like the raising of her heart rate or the trembling of her voice, she should just notice them, welcome them, and then focus on the counting again. Nina agreed to do so and started to observe her body.

She acknowledged and validated the steps in her process. She noticed her fear, welcomed it, and validated it. She noticed her explanation and welcomed it as just a story that was seeking her attention. She noticed the first step in the process, like and dislike. It just appeared and could be there without going further into reaction. As soon as like or dislike is there, it doesn't have to go or stay, it just has to be accepted.

Nina saw this clearly, and she experienced relief. She started the count and kept her full attention on the counting. She was standing in front of the group and was aware of the other participants. Whenever she was distracted by her bodily sensations, she just noticed them and brought her attention back to the counting. In a way the experience became more neutral. Nina counted loudly from 1 to 20 and kept her attention on the counting. It was the experience of her ability to shift her attention back to the counting again that made the change. The situation in itself had not changed, only her attention and attitude to the process had made a shift. She was no longer in an alert state, scanning her environment for possible threats to her self-image. She no longer feared rejection. She was just counting and keeping her focus on the counting task. Experiments like this have been performed numerous times in psychological labs, and the results are always the same. One can change the experience of social fear by changing the focus of attention to the task to be performed instead of allowing attention to scatter and listening to catastrophic stories in the head. Nina shifted her attention from the catastrophic stories in her head to observing and accepting her bodily sensations as they were while she was performing her counting task, and that was what made the shift for her. The bodily sensations are there. Just notice them and accept them. Nina was aware of the presence of the other participants and of her anticipatory thoughts of rejection as had happened several crucial times before in her life. Her behavior, thoughts, and emotional reactions followed a conditioned pattern. While avoiding social situations where she might be rejected, her thoughts justified her avoidance behavior. Minimizing the chances of rejection by avoiding confirmed her avoidance behavior. Her social fear pattern gained strength by avoiding risky social situations. As a professional psychotherapist, Nina knew the two-factor explanation of working factors in social fear. Minimizing the chance of negative consequences strengthens the conditioned avoidance patterns and weakens the development of social skills. She had even explained this theory to her students and patients and often stimulated them to practice these insights in their daily lives. We notice here that reasonable explanation and knowledge are insufficient teachers, and it is experience that creates the shift. In Nina's case, the experience of her fear of rejection, her sharing this with the other participants, and the experience of redirecting her attention from her social environment and catastrophic thoughts to the counting task itself neutralized her emotional reaction. The experience of her calmness and relief in a formerly risky situation made the change in her thoughts possible. Her mind told her not to participate in the proposed experiment and warned her of the potential damage to her self-image that could occur. She felt ashamed of her fear, and it was only after I motivated Nina to participate in the experiment that she reluctantly agreed and shared her fear with the others. The shift of attention gave her a real tool to cope with these social situations. Nina recognized this and started to practice this in her daily and professional life. Later on when we met at a conference, she stated that she had learned a lot from this experience, and social situations were far easier for her to handle. Though she still could experience her vulnerability to possible rejection, she now knew how to cope with it.

A writer's experiment with awareness

In this phase of the book I will start an experiment of my own, and I invite you as the reader to participate. Let's both shift our attention, you as a reader and I as a writer, to our own circle of awareness and explore where we meet. Let's use the circle of awareness to explore where our connection appears. We both know that the connection should be there, so let's use the circle to find it.

As a writer I write these words in a Moleskine notebook, a notebook reserved for the writing of this book. I write these words with a Parker pen that I got as a present from my wife as an encouragement and a token of her trust in this project. I write these words and I am aware of this writing, the moving of my pen on white lined paper. I am aware of the pauses in the writing. I write and just a split second later I read the words. Writing and reading are almost simultaneous. It resembles speaking and listening, where while I speak, I am aware of the words I speak. I notice the speaker inside me who speaks. It only takes a subtle shift of attention to become aware of the listener who listens to the words spoken. In fluent speaking, the speaker and the listener are present simultaneously while the thinker resides in the background. In fluent speaking, thinker and speaker seem to coincide. It is like thinking aloud. As I noticed on several occasions and then began to notice more and more, when I shift my attention to the listener inside myself, the listener seems to be more present. The first time I deliberately tried to make this shift in attention, I was surprised by the odd phenomena that occurred. It was like a revival of an old feeling that I experienced in my youth, a feeling of alienation that I disliked because it got me out of the connection with others and put me occasionally in a state of isolation. So while I was getting deeper into the awareness of the listener inside me, I had to overcome my initial reluctance to investigate this experience. From my professional background as a clinical psychologist, I know how patients get into a state of alienation as a natural defense against traumatic events. So what was happening to me when I voluntarily went into this state by shifting my attention from speaking to listening? Was I about to end up in a permanent state of dissociation as collateral damage on this awareness path I explored? Certainly not. When I continued to practice this shift of perspective from speaker to listener, I experienced more awareness and more presence. I became more aware of my body and of the stream of bodily sensations. People around me noticed this shift and stated that they experienced me as more present. Presence of what, one could ask. It was definitely not my ego or my mind. Something else was occurring, something more powerful and stronger than my mind could provoke; a present of awareness that was noticed by others and recognized as awareness. With this experience in my mind, I wonder what is happening right here and now in this writing process.

Me writing these words fluently while sitting at a table and using my pen to write down these words is like speaking fluently. I experience a curiosity for the next words that will flow from my pen. Breathing in, breathing out, with the sound of splashing water from the fountain falling in the pool outside, thoughts come into my mind. My here and now, my actual circle of awareness consists of a space where I am aware of me, as a person, writing these words, the sounds outside the room, and my body sitting on a chair near a table. The objects that come to my awareness are bygones and will disappear, and the sounds outside will be gone when these words come into print. The chair I am sitting on will not be there for the reader to sit on while reading these words. You as the reader and I as the writer are connected through these words and the meaning of these words. We don't share our outside world. Not even when I describe the momentary outside world of a pool with old Hindu statues as fountains for water to splatter into the pool. Palm trees fringe the pool. No one sits beside the pool. It is peaceful and quiet. Even when I describe the pool to you, the pool is not what connects us. The connection is formed through these words and their meaning. These words refer to awareness. You as a reader and I as a writer share a common interest in awareness.

Let's look at what we are aware of in this moment. For me as a writer there is only a vague notion of the words that are about to appear. As soon as I write them down I recognize these words as reasonable expressions of ideas that live inside me, ideas I share with numerous others around the world. I do not know which words are about to appear on the next page just as you, as a reader, do not know either. In this moment there is this reaching out for sharing ideas. So here we are on common ground with an awareness of a longing to share ideas. This moment is all there is, and we can only live in this moment. This moment has no true boundaries, just like any moment. Only the objects that appear in this moment, in the awareness of this moment, can come and go.

The subjective experience of me experiencing this moment will continue just as the subjective experience of your experiencing this moment will continue. Who is experiencing this moment? Out of habit I would say I am, but to be honest I don't know who is experiencing this moment.

The night after I wrote these words, I dreamed about an animated bicycle that caused a deadly accident for another cyclist. Still in the dream, while I tried to change the course of the dream events, a cloud of fear approached me. In that moment it became clear to me that the very root of my mind is seated in fear. It was clear to me that the dream was triggered by my question of what or who is hiding behind the bygones. The question itself terrified my mind, and it was as if my mind protested by eliciting this dream of an animated object, a bike that appeared like a sneaky monster on the road and caused an innocent cyclist to die in an accident. When I tried to change this dream, as I had learned to do in several dream workshops I attended decades ago, this cloud of fear arose. At that moment I labeled this cloud as a monster and accepted its appearance in my dream state. The monster first started to swell into a big, even more monstrous cloud, but then when I stayed calm and accepted its existence, it transformed into a harmless form. I woke up and found myself in a clear and lucid state of mind. There I was, lying in bed in a hotel room in Ubud, getting a night's sleep between classes of yoga I had been attending at the Yoga Barn. I sat in a yoga posture to calm my mind, and at that moment an insight in the form of a phrase came to me. 'All phenomena come from awareness and go to awareness.' All the bygones that are time and space limited phenomena emerge from awareness and vanish into awareness. I saw the vibrating ocean that all phenomena emerge from and disappear into again; an ocean of vibrating, dancing, living energy. The question I raised the day before while writing lines for this book detached a chain of reactions in my subconscious awareness as was now shown to me in this dream of an animated bike. Now it was clear to me that even fear comes from and goes into this ocean of awareness.

In a way, it is a fearful thought that everything that is around me in this moment, the whole context I am writing these words in, could disappear when in a future moment these words are read by a future reader. And again I realized how challenging it was for me to explore the connection between I as the writer and you as the reader of these words. Intuitively we both can know that the connection is there. I left the hotel room and went to write somewhere else.

Indeed it is possible that none of the objects or persons around me here in Ubud — now sitting at a table in the Yoga Barn on a Wednesday morning sometime in October 2013 — will exist when these words are read. When this whole context is gone, when only these words exist, what will be the connection? Is the connection still there and what will substantiate this connection? The form these words appear in will change. They will no longer appear in written letters on paper, instead they will probably appear in print on a page somewhere in a book still to be published. In this new form they will meet the eye of a formerly unknown reader without any mutual connection between writer and reader. This is of course a very familiar process, part of the daily routine of writing and reading. There is nothing really special here, yet still I notice this curiosity about what substantiates the connection between you as a reader and I as a writer. It reminds me of the connection between words and sound. We hear or read a word, and we know how to pronounce it. We are familiar with the sound of the word. Word and sound are connected. In between word and sound resides meaning. Meaning makes the word into a useful communication tool. In the case of a story the same is true. Meaning makes the connection between storyteller and story listener just as shared meaning is what makes the story an interesting one. The storyteller can play with meaning and the listener can follow this play and can become involved in the story. Common interest is what makes the story work. Common interest and shared meaning are all involved in storytelling. New stories will be invented and new listeners will be found. New stories will be written and new readers will be found.

Let's use this analogy to explore the connection between writer and reader. If all the bygones of this writing context are gone and only these words exist, what remains as a connection between writer and reader? Is common interest what makes the connection, a common interest in the topic at hand? Common interest will not last when the writer is gone, so what remains if the writer of these words is no longer here? What is the connection between writer and reader when the writer like all the other bygones is gone? Meaning can change over the course of time since it is certainly not a fixed phenomenon. In a way meaning is also part of bygones. So when none of the original aspects that are here as a form as I'm writing these words, what will remain when a future reader reads these words? The only thing that remains is awareness. We cannot call this a thing. When all objects are gone the only experience that remains is awareness. The only experience to experience is experience itself. This is what we call pure awareness. The connection between you as a reader and me as a writer is awareness. Awareness is floating between us, and we can both be curious about where this stream of awareness is taking us.

Behind all the bygones, awareness glimmers and expresses itself through bygones, playing its eternal play of awareness, reinventing itself over and over. When we place our self in our own daily circle of awareness, we have to look behind the phenomena to see that it all emerges from the same source, awareness. This is a connection that is shown in the thought experiment about the connection between writer and reader. Through the limits of space and time we can experience mutual awareness.

This book is an open invitation to self-exploration. You can start reading at any page and whenever you like, and you can step in and out of the circle whenever you want. There is only one precondition — as soon as you step into the circle, you let your self-exploration start. The same with this book, you can start at any page and allow the hidden awareness in this book to happen. Simply ask yourself while you are reading these words what you are aware of. What are the sounds around you? What is the posture of your body? Are you aware of the breathing in and breathing out? Can you observe the rising and falling of your thoughts? What are you aware of? This simple question is all it takes to start the process of self-exploration. What are you aware of in this moment? Maybe you notice a distraction while reading this, something asking for your attention. Just allow it to be there and decide when you want to give it your attention. Notice how something longs for your attention, whatever it is, and decide in your own time and space when you want to give it your attention.

What you and I connect in is awareness. Awareness is what is communicating between us. Awareness is telling us something, awareness brings insight. There are no final answers to be found, no final conclusions to write down. We are witnessing awareness reinventing itself and communicating between us.

Eating awareness

Mindfullness means paying attention in a particular way,
on purpose, in the present moment, non-judgmentally.
(Jon Kabat-Zinn)

How about eating? What happens with our eating when we add awareness to eating? Eating is definitely a part of daily routine. If you add awareness to eating, the quality of your eating will improve. Your eating will become more tasteful, more fulfilling, and more satisfying. You will enjoy your eating. What happens if you add thinking to your eating? Your thinking will comment on everything you eat and drink. And then what will happen? Your taste will become less outspoken, less subtle, more flat and coarse. If you add thinking to eating, you multitask in a complicated way. You try to eat and think at the same time. Thinking wants your attention and claims to be of utmost importance. Thinking will soon discover that what and how you eat might be harmful for you. For example, you start thinking that you eat too much or take in too many calories, so then you think you have to change what you eat. Thinking anticipates the future and decides that you have to change how and what you eat. An odd paradox arises here. While eating, thinking is claiming so much attention that the awareness of eating goes to the background and eating is performed routinely without the necessary ingredient to make your eating a joyful experience. You no longer experience your eating, you experience the effect of your thoughts that interfere with the eating experience. Mindful eating is not an effort at all, thoughtful eating is.

While you eat, try not to think. Instead of thinking about your eating, try to experience the eating. Use your senses before food comes into your mouth. Smell the food, see the food, and taste the food. Notice the texture of the food entering your mouth. Take your time with this and experience the mixture of sensations. Don't overload. If you overload, you will miss the variation in sensations.

From working with obese patients I have learned a profound lesson. I was curious about what caused these patients to overload their digestive systems, and it appears that many of these obese patients are emotional eaters. They use eating as a way to deal with emotional distress and to comfort themselves with the good and pleasant feeling caused by eating. By eating they were compensating for unpleasant feelings like sadness or fear. This is something that works very well at that moment, but in the long run it causes serious negative side effects of obesity. Compensation for emotional distress is quite a popular psychological explanation for overeating, but of course this explanation is too flat and too simple to explain the complexity of overeating behavior. Numerous psychological, biological, and cultural factors are necessary to explain the complexity of this self-destructive addictive behavior. We all want to feel comfortable and experience good feelings. There is a vast preference for feeling good. We don't get out of bed in the morning and instruct ourselves to start another unhappy day, we hope for a happy day. If unhappiness appears, eating is an instantaneous cure for this unhappy feeling. Eating is truly a way to create pleasure in the moment.

In the long explorative meetings I had with these patients, I noticed that something else was happening too. There was something at the very start of the overeating impulse, something so strong that it needed to be avoided or escaped from, and something that is so obvious that it is easily overlooked because it is part of a vast, conditioned behavioral pattern. Through the day between our meals, we experience all kinds of internal cues. If we take the time to experience our stomach and digestive system, we notice space inside the stomach and digestive system. This is a subtle cue that accompanies the freedom of movement in our belly. We cannot experience the absence of this space, instead we experience a full stomach or full belly. The experience of the full belly is easy to notice. The absence of this fullness is a feeling of emptiness in the stomach and belly. This feeling of emptiness is intolerable for obese patients. The inner space has to be filled up until they are completely fulfilled. This feeling lasts only a short time and the process of filling up continues. If they experience this feeling of emptiness in their stomach, this feeling is labeled negatively and it needs to be avoided. Instantaneously the urge to fill up appears and is acted upon. All of these patients were able to follow a strict diet and could even fast for a considerable period of time. During fasting and dieting they experienced strong feelings, and they suffered a lot by withholding their usual food intake. They praised themselves for their courageous attempts but never learned to label the experience of emptiness as positive and even joyful. This is not what they learned from their own experience. Then a relapse in their old eating pattern easily occurred. The metaphor we discovered in the conversations with obese patients is the metaphor of a comfortable living room. You need space to enjoy the comfort of the furniture. If the room is completely filled up, you can't live in it. This is also true with food. We need emptiness to digest it. So as we eat in our daily routine, we should add awareness to it. We should give attention to the space around the food, experience the sensations, smell, taste, and texture of the food. We should notice how the food is accommodating to the space in your mouth, how you swallow it through your gullet, and how it finds its way to your stomach. We should notice that there is still space left, and experience the emptiness. As we need silence in music, we need space around food to experience the unique mixture of sensations from the food in that moment.

We should eat in such a way that when we leave the table we experience a slight and subtle urge. That is how you experience this emptiness in your belly, a slight, tingling, buzzing feeling of emptiness. It is a vivid experience. If your mind tries to control your diet, you will start to dislike your eating and feel guilty because you fail to fulfill the standards your mind has set for eating. Your mind will make it a problem as it does with everything.

Sleep awareness

Sleep is the best meditation. (Dalai Lama)

All daily routines need to be conditioned, according to the mind, so that you are no longer surprised by the novelty of events but can feel comfortable with the routine repetition of events. Eating, sleeping, and sex are vital activities for your daily life. When sleeping becomes a problem, your mind has a simple but sadly ineffective solution: more thinking, and you find yourself fully awake in bed, thinking a lot and especially about how to go to sleep. Your body tries every possible posture and still sleep doesn't come. All kinds of issues pass by and you keep thinking about them. This is a truly uncomfortable situation and you will find yourself longing for a good night's sleep, you will keep thinking about how to get to sleep. In this case, the solution is the problem. You can't switch off the thinking. Whenever several processes occur simultaneously and one of them is thinking, thinking will claim all the attention. The thinking process is a strong competitor and knows how to get attention. Whatever gets the attention will survive and last longer. For processes like sleeping, eating, and sex, thinking is the most prominent and successful competitor to become a true attention winner. You can't stop thinking, but you can shift attention. Sleeping is a process of the body, and the body has no need for the supervising mind to control the sleeping. So if sleeping is a process of the body, then the body itself is where the attention should go, for instance by observing your breathing in and breathing out. Follow this with your attention focused on the movement of your breath through your body; just notice and don't change it and whenever you are distracted by your thoughts, just bring your attention back to the movement of your breath. This can be a little bit confusing for your mind. Your mind could comment that this is a form of meditation and while meditating you should stay alert and awake to notice all the experiences that are there to experience. Meditating indeed calms the mind by following the breath and observing what is there to observe. Now you can use this technique of shifting your attention away from the thinking process to allow your body to take over and fall asleep. You can also observe how your body touches the mattress and focus on the interface between your body and mattress. Just observe it as it is, a neutral experience that is just happening without any mind control. The experience is just there. Don't interfere with it and your body will know how to fall asleep.

The day starts with waking up. You find yourself lying in bed and you wake up. You become aware of your body in your bed. Your busy mind starts buzzing with the agenda for the day. Your mind takes over and you are no longer aware of your body. Maybe you remember all the things that need to be done and that you have not yet accomplished. You rush to the toilet, shower, eat breakfast, and hurry to start the day. Maybe you feel a little bit tired, but you ignore that because there is so much that needs to be done.

Amanda took part in the mindfulness group for psychotherapists in training, a five-day retreat. One morning during the opening meeting, she said she had woken up in a sad mood that day. At that moment she had realized that while she felt very happy and accepted in the group, in a few days she would return home to lead her single life again. We explored with Amanda how she usually woke up and asked her to demonstrate her waking up routine. A mattress was put on the floor in the middle of the circle. Amanda lay down and showed how she would immediately throw her body out of the bed as soon as she opened her eyes. She treated her body as a piece of garbage that she threw out of the bed and then rushed through her daily routine of a single working woman. She was hardly aware of how self-destructive her waking up routine actually was. I asked Amanda to repeat this waking up process but now in a mindful way. I asked her to wake up and feel her body lying in the bed and feel how the energy moves through her body and asked her to wait for the impulse to open her eyes and move her limbs, wait for the impulse to move her legs out of the bed, and observe the moving of her body. Amanda did so, and we saw how she became aware of her body and then how her arms and legs gently started to move. She opened her eyes with a smile on her face. Self-positive thoughts entered her mind. She experienced a positive and tender awakening. The process was simple, but the change Amanda underwent was profound. Later when we met at a conference, Amanda explained that she had kept this routine of mindful awakening and had found her life in a positive flow again.

Experiencing her change in mood and thought is what made Amanda incorporate this change into her daily routine. By adding awareness to a daily routine and observing and accepting what changes appear, deconditioning can take place. Awareness in itself floats and changes all the time, and it is not busy consolidating the good or condemning the bad. Awareness is just floating around and accepting what is. It never holds onto anything and it never resists anything. In this state of awareness and accep-

tance, beneficial changes can occur. It is indeed of great importance to use our daily life as an experiential laboratory for
awareness.

Awareness and love

Love is the natural condition of all experience before thought
has divided it into a multiplicity and diversity of objects, selves
and others. (Rupert Spira)

What constitutes an intimate relationship? What do intimates
experience in intimacy? What is communicated between intimates? What do they validate in each other? Do intimates make
plans about how to furnish their home? Yes, they do. Together
they create a nice environment. They make plans about future
changes etc. What does that planning do for them? It generates
good feelings. An intimate relationship is all about sharing good
feelings. First we have to acquire the ability to experience good
and comfortable feelings in ourselves before we can offer such
feelings in an intimate relationship. We exchange feelings in an
intimate relationship. An intimate relationship is primarily a
small community of shared feelings and not of thoughts. Instead
of asking, 'Do you love me?' one should ask, 'Do you feel me?'
Feeling is what it's all about. When the feelings are gone, the intimacy is gone. Intimates should never stop feeling. Even if you feel
irritated, that's fine; irritation is still a feeling. Notice it in yourself, accept your irritation, and contain it. Notice the irritation of
your partner as you noticed your own. Notice, name it, and con-

tain it. Just let irritation be there. Label it as just one of the feelings you share in your intimate feeling community. Validate the irritation of your intimate as you validate a feeling of joy. Validate your mutual feelings; welcome them in your intimate emotional community.

Sleeping, eating, and relating form major parts of our daily lifes. So let's look into what many of us consider as the most important, relating. One could say it all starts with relating since we are born in a relationship, we grow up in relationship. We develop in the caring relationship of our mother, father, and siblings. Our self-image is the product of the relational dynamics in which we grew up. Our life begins in a relationship. As we have seen, our daily lives are subject to conditioning, as are our relationships. Our social self is formed in our family and further modified in our peer group. We learn to adapt to the likes and dislikes of significant others in our social environment. Not all of us are so lucky as to be raised in a loving and caring family. Many of us, if not all of us, were not accepted unconditionally, even though the (loving) care we received was unavoidably part of a conditioning process. As we shall see, it is this conditioned self that hinders us in acquiring a loving spouse. Relating in daily life starts with self-relating, an encounter with your authentic, unconditioned self. This authentic self is neutral, and you hardly notice it because you are so used to it. It accompanies you everywhere you go. In this self is where your true intimacy is. It is here that self-acceptance and self-compassion can emerge. No one else is able to experience your life as you do. You are truly the only experiential expert of your own life. This has nothing to do with a bundle of features or special qualities you have acquired during your life and modified in your social environment. This is about the intimate experience of being you. It is the intimate experience with your own bodily sensations, feelings, and thoughts. What are you aware of while you experience these intimate experiences? That is the first step in self-acceptance. What are the bodily sensations, feelings, and thoughts you are aware of? Self-acceptance doesn't start as an idea but as the acceptance of your own intimate experiences. We start by adding awareness to our intimate experiences. We add awareness to the meeting of our neutral self. We start by asking ourselves what we are aware of. Which bodily sensations come to our awareness? Which feelings, which thoughts appear? Maybe you notice that even in this domain, thought claims the floor. Thought claims to be of the utmost importance and says that our meeting with another person needs to be thought over thoroughly. Let's put thought into the background and give the floor to the body. What do we notice when we pay attention to our bodily sensations, when we are aware of our breathing in and breathing out while we meet this other person? When we no longer listen to the other with our thoughts but with our ears, what happens? What happens when we hear the sound of the voice of the other? Instantaneously like and dislike will appear, approach and avoidance will appear. The potential intimate other is not someone to be thought of but someone to be experienced through our bodily sensations. We experience the presence of the other, but this can only occur if we can experience ourselves as we are in our neutral state, become aware of our own neutral and normal bodily sensations, and accept them as they are. In taking care of your body you will become more aware of your body. It is through your body that you will experience the intimate other, so you need to get consciously familiar with your own body. Become aware of your bodily sensations and accept them as they are. Accept your weight, the color of your hair, the shape of your body, the way it moves and the smell of your skin. Accept it all as it is. Experience your own attractiveness and present this to others. Don't hide anything; between intimates there are no secrets. Secrets are mind stuff. As there are no secrets from your intimate self, there are no secrets from your intimate other. If you aim for true intimacy, there is no place for secrets. It all starts with self-acceptance, not as a compensation for inferiority feelings but as a true discovery of your authentic self and your unconditional self-acceptance. Then the room for an intimate other emerges. And of course you are curious as to the otherness of the intimate other. Indeed the intimate other is truly someone other than yourself and is truly someone else. How is it possible that the intimate other is so familiar and yet so foreign? You can only wonder how that is possible. You don't know the otherness of the intimate other as you know the features of an object. This is not a cognitive endeavor, it is an experiential experience. The intimate other can only be experienced, the intimate other is not to be known. You are aware of the intimate experience, you experience intimacy with the other, and you know you experience this intimacy with the other. You know in a very intimate way the presence of the intimate other and still you don't know the other. You can be amazed and astonished about how someone can come so close to you and still remain so unknown. How can someone be so familiar and yet so strange? You cannot predict the next step of the intimate other and yet you know that you will unconditionally accept it. Intimacy is party time for your body. Your body likes the proximity of an intimate other. A true symphony of a lot of liking and little disliking.

Strange things happen when we add awareness to our lives and allow awareness to fulfill what wants to be fulfilled. As we open up to awareness itself and experience ourselves as truly living beings, accepting everything that comes into our awareness and trusting in whatever we experience, life will surprise us later on with something good that is about to happen.

You long for another person, yet unknown, and yet you are sure that this person is about to come into your life. In your heart you already experience the closeness with that other person. This is what happens with women seeking treatment for involuntary infertility. Their child wish is so strong that they seek treatment with in vitro fertilization (IVF). At the hospital where I work we offer mindfulness group training for women in IVF treatment. The results of mindfulness training with IVF patients are similar to the results of the training for cardiac patients. As with cardiac patents, IVF patients suffer from mood disturbances, and the training focuses on accepting the child wish as it is. The unfulfilled child wish is like an emotional roller coaster. These women see pregnant women everywhere, and they feel ashamed that they cannot fulfill the expectations of themselves and significant others. Their child wish can easily transform into a child demand. How to cope with these strong feelings is an important question for them. At the hospital we know from our research that women who undergo regular medical infertility treatment will experience negative effects in their mood and quality of life, and they will develop mood disturbances to a greater or lesser extent. The cultural way to approach this unfulfilled child wish is medical and cognitive, and in many cases that is enough and successful. If the child wish is fulfilled, it is worth the effort. These newborns are very welcome, and it is a blessing for the many subfertile women that IVF treatment is possible. But this medical and cognitive approach sadly enough leads to unnecessary collateral damage as we noticed through our research.

The results of the mindfulness training we offer at the hospital in conjunction with the regular medical treatment are very encouraging. The women who join the group remain emotionally stable and even slightly improve their quality of life. The group training follows the basic steps of learning to observe bodily sensations, emotions, and thoughts. Much attention is given to developing a self-compassionate attitude while carrying this unfulfilled child wish. Longing for an unborn child is like longing for a lover, because they are both a matter of the heart. The mind does not understand the slightest thing about it, the mind is simply not equipped for this. When we ask the participants of the group where they experience the presence of their child wish in their body, they all point to their hearts. That's the place where we teach them to seek comfort while living this unfulfilled child wish. The heart knows how to manage and the mind should not interfere. Self-compassion is of great importance in this matter. The child wish starts as a warm and joyful feeling in the heart, and that's where the wish should live. Don't let your mind with its doubts distract you from that warm and joyful feeling in your heart. Live the child wish from your heart. If people ask if a child is on the way, simply reply that a child is very welcome whenever it decides to come. Unconditional love is what parents practice while raising their child. This practice starts with the yet unfulfilled child wish. In the group we teach participants in role plays how to cope with these questions and experience how an accepting, heartful response heals the emotional wounds caused by frustration. In a way there is nothing special the women have to do, just open their hearts and allow the wish to be there, create a heartful welcome for the unknown child, and accept whenever it decides to come. One case dramatically illustrates the strength of this accepting attitude versus the ever doubtful and worrying attitude of the mind.

Nancy, a woman in her midthirties, was referred to me with premature meno-pause, meaning that she was medically infertile and could not fulfill her child wish. We had a conversation about how to cope with this dramatic shift in her life perspective and how to accept her feelings of despair and sadness and develop a self-compassionate attitude. We had a warm and comforting conversation, and I was impressed by the strength Nancy demonstrated in our meeting. Several weeks later she came to me for her next appointment, and she was extremely surprised. She announced that she was pregnant. It was a true miracle, and she was full of joy and gratitude. Then her mind shifted. During the session she started to worry. Her mind could not handle this new situation, and it raised all kinds of doubts. That's what the mind always does if it can't understand a new event. The mind pulled her out of the actual moment. Fortunately it was easy to make the connection with her heart again and let her heart handle this miracle. For her heart, it was a truly hap-py and loving experience, and we concluded that her heart would know how to car-ry and raise her child.

Awareness and erotic intimacy

They slipped briskly into an intimacy from which they never
recovered. (F. Scott Fitzgerald)

We saw how relating is improved if we add awareness to it. How
about a sexual encounter? Does adding awareness improve sexual encounters? Wouldn't that be nice? Happily your sex life will
improve if you add awareness. When making love one could
wonder who is making love. Who is doing it? The simple answer
would be: I am. I am having the sex, I am making love. I am loving
it. If there is any domain in which overidentification with an ac-
tivity is at stake, it is in our sexual behavior. Overidentification
with sexual behavior is a serious obstacle for sexual intimacy. In
my medical sexology practice I see patients with sexual dysfunc-
tions. Among sexologists, it is widely known how people suffer
from sexual performance anxiety. People do their best to have a
good sexual performance. In intimate sexual encounters the risk
of self-damage is high. In these kinds of intimate encounters,
people experience themselves as vulnerable. It is precisely this
vulnerability that is a precondition for true intimacy. The same is
true for self-exposure. You show yourself in all your nakedness to
your intimate lover, and that's where the risk of rejection is the

highest. Sexual intimacy is part of the emotional relating process. You become very close with your sexual partner. As I learned from my patients and also from my own experiences, sexual behavior in itself is not complicated at all. It should be no problem at all. In my practice I have learned to articulate more explicitly the non-problematic side of sexual intimacy. Sexual intimacy can be a very pleasant and satisfying form of human behavior. It can be, but for most people it isn't. Many people make love with a busy, crowded mind, an anxious heart, and a cramped body. Trouble begins when the mind takes over. Anticipatory performance anxiety dictates the intimate encounter, and disappointment and shame are the result. The mind does not know how to be intimate. The mind knows all about self-protection and nothing whatsoever about true self-disclosure. The mind tries to avoid vulnerable situations and if that's impossible, tries to control them. The fearful mind tries to dominate the sexual encounter with reversed effect, namely lack of intimacy. The recipe for a nice and good sexual intimate encounter is simple: an empty mind, a full heart, and a flexible body. The body knows how to express and share sexual arousal. The heart knows how to love. Leave your mind out of it. This is a simple recipe and sometimes very hard to follow. If we ask the thinker not to think, the thinker will think about it. We can't ask the mind to stop thinking during sex but we can ask the lover to shift attention to the body and experience sexual arousal as it comes and goes. It is a floating energy, rising and blossoming in the belly. Just experience this floating vibrating energy and let it inspire you. Your body and your lover's body know how to express and live in this energy. It is like a sexual dance, inventing itself over and over again, with every moment as a new moment, every experience as a new experience. There is nothing to anticipate, just let the heartful body play. Don't do anything deliberately and let it occur fluently. Undo the doing. Don't do the sex, let the sex do you. Just experience the dance of sexual arousal. Who is making love, you might wonder? For sure it is not you, nor is it she or he. Neither of you is making love, love is making you. Love is dancing with love, love is dancing with the sexual energy. Then there is nothing of importance that needs to be done by you.

Lovers merge with each other and lose themselves. They lose themselves in the experience of 'we.' You and I dissolve in 'we.' The separate self dissolves in the ocean of 'we.' In 'we,' I no longer exist. The separate self, this so-called I, yearns for connection, yearns to dissolve itself.

What is left is the awareness of this merging together. The separate self no longer exists. It surrenders itself to love and sexual arousal. But what about the mind? We know from numerous experiences that the mind is very busy with sex. The mind knows the pleasure of sex and is eager to create sexually stimulating situations. Sex is overloaded with meaning, and meaning is the domain of the mind. The mind will not allow itself to be put off to the side about such an important issue. The mind will claim a prominent role. What should we do with this interfering mind? Let's look for a more suitable task for the mind. Let's use this issue of sex to validate the mind with a new and more appropriate task. Let the mind flourish with the body and heart in this vital sexual intimate experience. Let the mind experience its true nature, experiment with it by applying it in daily life. The core quality of mind is to serve. The mind should go on with this important task, only the mind needs to serve another master. The mind is conditioned to serve the illusionary separate self; it is exactly this kind of self that dissolves in the intimate sexual encounter. It is exactly this self that longs for dissolving itself and to end the separation. This separate self doesn't need a servant anymore. We give the mind a new task and a new master: awareness. Let the mind serve awareness with one simple task, bring like and dislike to the attention of awareness. Let awareness float around like and dislike. Let your mind make this profound shift and start serving awareness instead of serving an illusionary separate self. In intimacy we long to merge with the intimate other, and our awareness of the connection with the intimate other flourishes, undoing the doing and making space for loving awareness.

Attend to how the sexual energy rises in your body, notice how this energy knows how to move and float through your body. Notice how this energy takes over, and let your mind notice the sensation of this energy taking over. Notice how your body seems almost too small to contain all of this energy, how this energy reaches out for your lover, and how both of you merge in this ocean of sexual energy. It is a symphony of simultaneous exchange of sexual energy. Notice the rising and falling of this energy and experience this timeless moment where you are no longer there as a separate self. There is only the awareness of we. Where we begins, You and I end.

Practicing awareness in daily life

Give your attention to the experience of seeing, rather than to
the object seen and you will find yourself everywhere.
(Rupert Spira)

The real practice is in practicing awareness in daily life. Just add
awareness to whatever you are doing in daily life. And start playing with awareness, don't take it too seriously. Awareness in itself
is neutral and non-judgmental. Just pay attention to whatever
comes to your awareness. You become aware of something by
bringing your attention to it. As soon as it is there you can only
accept it as it is. It is already there, just as it is. In accepting it as it
is, an opportunity for change will appear, so start with whatever
comes spontaneously to your awareness, let it be a thought or a
feeling. Just observe it entering your awareness, and simultaneously bring your attention to a neutral process in your body. You
can choose the movement of your breath in your body. You can
feel this movement in your nostrils, your chest or belly. It doesn't
matter where you focus your attention while breathing, just let
the movement of your breathing go as it goes. You don't need to
improve this movement in any way. Your body knows how to
breathe, and while observing the neutral movement of the breath
you develop a neutral stance. It is this neutral stance you need to

become more aware of in order to profit from the beneficial changes awareness has in mind for you, so to speak.

Something is entering your awareness and is seeking your attention, so now you can decide what kind of attention you are about to give. We can distinguish two kinds of attention. Absorption attention, in which you are absorbed by the object that is entering your awareness and you can no longer distance from it. You are not able to observe neutrally, and you can't see what is actually happening. This kind of attention is like Velcro since your attention is tied and fixed like a Velcro strip. The other form of attention is closer attention. With this kind of attention, you approach the object and yet keep a slight distance. This attention is like Teflon because your attention is close to the object and yet not attached to it. Your attention glides along the object, thought, or feeling. Developing neutral and closer attention is one of the core skills needed to become more aware. During the day there are numerous activities where you can practice this. You train this skill by observing a neutral process in the body like the movement of your breathing, and then you apply this skill to other objects entering your awareness. Whatever you do, add awareness to it and notice what happens. You can start in the morning when you wake up. Just observe your body in the bed. Notice the contact between your body and the mattress, and observe the impulse of moving your body to get up out of bed. Observe how this impulse grows. Let it grow by itself and merge into action, then observe the rising of your body.

Daily life consists of numerous routines — sleeping, bodily needs, housekeeping, socializing, work etc. — activities that can more or less be fulfilled in a routine way. And there is nothing wrong with that. Routines are practical and consume less energy than developing new behavioral patterns. They do on the other hand show us how easily one can be absorbed by conditioned patterns and thereby lose your sense of authenticity and liveliness. Practicing routine behavior it is just as if life has lost its splendor. The mind develops conditioned behavioral patterns as a means to make you comfortable and protect you from future harm. The mind is there to serve you, so the mind organizes your life and collects material objects like comfortable clothes and furniture. The mind creates and follows behavioral routines. The mind is not aiming for prosperity in itself, it uses wealth and well-being as instruments for creating comfort and protecting you from future harm.

How does awareness float through daily life? Awareness is always there and will always stay. This doesn't mean that you have to notice the presence of awareness like the air you are breathing. Just because your breathing is always there, it doesn't mean that you notice the breathing. Air is present in and outside you like awareness is. Awareness is all around you. It is impossible for us to experience the absence of awareness. We can observe the absence of awareness in others or retrospectively conclude the absence of awareness in ourselves, for example when we are sleeping. We can thus conclude the absence of awareness at that time, but still we have no experience of the absence of awareness. Awareness is only to be approached metaphorically. There is no direct language for the experience of awareness. Awareness lacks distinguishable features, and the experience of awareness cannot be described in common language. We can approach the experience with metaphors like endless space, but still this metaphor is not the experience itself.

We can conclude that awareness was absent for instance when we drive from A to B and suddenly find ourselves at a point on the route and realize we are unaware that we have already been there. You were unaware for a period of time and did not experience driving on the road. Routine behavioral patterns take over, and your mind concludes that your awareness was absent. Maybe your attention was drifting away in daydreaming or was filled with thoughts about what to eat that evening, but your attention was not focused in the here and now. In the absence of your awareness of breathing, it is odd to conclude that your breathing has stopped. Breathing is a continuous process and will continue even when you don't think about it, as in routine driving. The absence of consciously noticing that you are driving does not mean that you have stopped driving. In the absence of thinking about the driving process, the driving can just go on. The absence of thinking of driving does not imply the absence of driving. The absence of thoughts doesn't imply the absence of awareness.

Routine behavior like driving happens throughout daily life. In practicing routine behavior awareness seems to be absent, and we recognize immediately the return to a clear state of awareness. In that very moment, we experience that we are aware. Experiencing something, whatever it is, implies awareness. Awareness and experience come together. Experience in itself doesn't come or go, it is our thinking that does. In the absence of thinking, pure awareness and experience appear.

So how can this approach to awareness be handy in daily life? The examples you read in this book are there to inspire you. You can experiment with them and modify them for your own personal use. These examples are not there to be replicated exactly as they are. They won't fit you as they did the participants of the circle who raised the issue. No form will last forever. If an example appeals to you, just let it resonate inside you and see what insight it brings you. Your mind will start to look for conclusions and explanations while reading the examples in this book. Just allow your mind to do so, and be unreservedly friendly towards your mind since it has no easy task in this world and it fulfils this task with the best of intentions, to protect you from harm. So be very friendly to this protector of yours and just add awareness to it.

Practicing awareness in your daily life starts with awareness of your bodily sensations. Then add a neutral stance to these sensations and just observe the sensations as they are. Notice the likeability and unlikeability, and, if necessary, change whatever is needed to make your body comfortable. Just add awareness to your act of change. For instance, you sit on a chair and notice a stiffness in your leg. Just move your leg and notice how your leg feels comfortable again. By the nature of your body, your body seeks a comfortable posture. Your body likes to feel fluid instead of rigid. Whenever an uncomfortable stimulus enters your awareness, your body will try to escape from it. If that's not possible, your body will freeze in that posture. If this freeze response goes on too long, your body will memorize this posture in your fascia. It is in your fascia that rigid postures are memorized and repeated. If you would like to have a flexible body, add yin yoga exercises to your daily routines. A yin yoga practice is a good way to unfreeze your body.

Be very compassionate with your thoughts and mind. While practicing this compassionate and accepting stance, your mind will calm down. And from time to time, an emptiness in your mind will appear. Be aware of this empty mind state and note the easiness of these moments. Life seems to float and live by itself. It is in this self-compassionate state that you can meet your neutral and authentic self, and it is in this compassionate state that the connection with your loved ones is almost tangible. Thoughts about your intimate other enter your mind and your body will react to them. But even before these thoughts are there, there is the knowing of the connection, a connection that resides in your awareness. In your awareness you know of the connection with your loved ones. There, in your awareness, there is no room for misunderstanding. You know the connection is there.

Live your life with an empty mind, a full heart, and a yoga body.

It all starts with the experience of you, your body, thoughts, and feelings. In accepting you as you are at that moment, room for change can appear. Whatever you resist in yourself will persist. Whatever you accept will continue and or transform and your awareness will grow and you can build your own circle of awareness where you can watch you. Intimate others can enter your sphere of awareness because your circle has sufficient room.

Awareness has nothing to win or lose. It is just there waiting for you to allow it to grow. You can take your time. There is no hurry at all. Awareness can grow, most certainly, but it is not aiming for that at all. Awareness can grow in wisdom and still awareness is not aiming for that either. Awareness is just playing with awareness, inventing itself over and over again in numerous plays.

Afterword

The circle of awareness was first introduced in 2005 as an experiential form of group psychotherapy for cognitive behavioral psychotherapists in training. The circle is a modification of an experiential group training format called the Forum, developed by the Zegg community in Germany. The basic form of the circle of awareness is the same as this Forum where people sit in a circle with one of the participants exploring an issue while getting instructions from the trainer and feedback from the group. I attended several training weekends in the Zegg community, and I'm still very grateful for the inspiration I received from those weekends. At Venwoude in the Netherlands we worked with this Forum form, and I was lucky to learn my first Forum steps there with a lot of very enthusiastic participants and trainers. Another root of the circle lies in Vipassana meditation. I'm deeply touched by the profound insights I gained from several Vipassana retreats. These two roots are integrated in the cognitive behavioral group psychotherapy I have been offering since 2005. As a result I have developed the Circle of Awareness as a core method for this group psychotherapy for cognitive behavioral psychotherapists in training. The cognitive behavioral method I used in this group psychotherapy is known as COMET or counter conditioning. This method was introduced in the Netherlands by prof Kees Korrelboom.

Since the introduction of the circle, I have facilitated several hundred groups using this form with an average of eight participants in each group and a range from six to twenty-five participants. I introduced the circle as an open and free monthly group training at Aquamarijn in Eindhoven, the Netherlands, where participants could join the group and step in and out as often as they liked. In a reduced form, I used the method of the circle at the Catharina Hospital in Eindhoven as a part of mindfulness training for cardiac and IVF patients.

The stories in this book are constructed from experiences with these various groups. The characters have been made anonymous and resemblance with real persons is based on coincidence. The experiences described in this book are based on true stories of participants, and my hope is that these stories can inspire readers to further their practice of awareness.

This book could never have been published without the help of friends. Bridget and Carrie, thank you very much for editing the text and transforming my Dutch English into real English. Jasper, your sharp and supportive comments were a great help to me to come to a round circle. Joska, thank you for your supportive and warm comments. Joris, thank you for your advice on the book design. All the participants of the circle, I thank you all for the inspiration you gave for a deeper understanding of what we all share, awareness.

Finally, but not least, Sultana my beloved wife and muse. You read all my words, and we discussed our insights on awareness and applied them in our training group. This book reflects our work as mindfulness trainers and our love for this work.